Communication Skills for Couples

2 Manuscripts in 1 book

Mindful Relationship Habits for Couples + Communication Skills for Couples: No More Conflict! A Practical Guide to Improve Mindful Habits and Empathic Listening

© Copyright 2019 by _____ - All rights reserved.

This eBook is provided with the sole purpose of providing relevant information on a specific topic for which every reasonable effort has been made to ensure that it is both accurate and reasonable. Nevertheless, by purchasing this eBook, you consent to the fact that the author, as well as the publisher, are in no way experts on the topics contained herein, regardless of any claims as such that may be made within. As such, any suggestions or recommendations that are made within are done so purely for entertainment value. It is recommended that you always consult a professional before undertaking any of the advice or techniques discussed within.

This is a legally binding declaration that is considered both valid and fair by both the Committee of Publishers Association and the American Bar Association and should be considered as legally binding within the United States.

The reproduction, transmission, and duplication of any of the content found herein, including any specific or extended information will be done as an illegal act regardless of the end form the information ultimately takes. This includes copied versions of the work both physical, digital and audio unless express consent of the Publisher is provided beforehand. Any additional rights reserved.

Furthermore, the information that can be found within the pages described forthwith shall be considered both accurate and truthful when it comes to the recounting of facts. As such, any use, correct or incorrect, of the provided information will render the Publisher free of responsibility as to the actions taken outside of their direct purview. Regardless, there are zero scenarios where the original author or the Publisher can be deemed liable in any fashion for any damages or hardships that may result from any of the information discussed herein.

Additionally, the information in the following pages is intended only for informational purposes and should thus be thought of as universal. As befitting its nature, it is presented without assurance regarding its continued validity or interim quality. Trademarks that are mentioned are done without written consent and can in no way be considered an endorsement from the trademark holder.

Communication for Couples

Introduction 10
Chapter 1: What is empathy? 11
Chapter 2: Empathic Listening (Using Empathy to listen to your partner) 15
   Empathy: the cornerstone of authentic human interactions 17
   What is empathic listening? 17
   How does empathic listening relate to happiness? 18
   Empathic listening for couples 18
   Empathic listening at work 19
   How to practice empathic listening? 20
   9 strategies to develop empathic listening 21
   The importance of empathic listening 24
   Strategies to develop empathetic listening 24
   In summary: 25
Chapter 3: The importance of work on yourself first 26
   Causes of conflicts between couples 26
   How to deal with anger 27
   Communication as a cornerstone to work on yourself 27
      Verbal communication between couples 28
      Nonverbal communication between couples 29
   Physical acts 29
Chapter 4: Diplomatic dialogue skills 31
Chapter 5: Mindful Habits 38
   Common practices of healthy couples 38
Chapter 6: Appreciating and Accepting your Partner 41
   Tips on how to accept your partner for who they are in a committed relationship 41
   Appreciating your partner in a relationship 43
      Signs showing that your partner is not feeling appreciated in a relationship 44
      Ways of showing your partner that you appreciate them 45
      Importance of showing appreciation to your spouse 45
   Replacing judgment with compassion in a relationship 46
Chapter 7: The Ego Monster 47
   Signs of egoism in a relationship 47

How ego can kill a relationship.. 48
   One's ego can ruin a conversation with your spouse 49
   Signs showing that ego is destroying your relationship 49
How to control your ego and improve your relationship 50
The battle of love versus ego 51
   How the battle unfolds 51
How you can deal with a person with a huge ego 52

Chapter 8: Love Unconditionally 53
Romantic unconditional love 53
Positive unconditional love 53
How to love unconditionally 53
How to know that you have found unconditional love 54
   Unconditional love does not mean you are there no matter what you do 55
   Unconditional love is not being codependent 55
   Unconditional love is not all about your partner 55
   Unconditional love does not mean over-protecting your partner 56
   True unconditional love allows a couple to change and grow as individuals overtime 56
   Unconditional love is not one -way 57
Relationship break down 57
Conditional love vs. unconditional love 58

Chapter 9: Set Goals for Your Relationship 60
What are these couple relationship goals? 60
Relationship goals for couples to nurture and protect their bond 61
Long-term relationship goals 63
Reasons for setting common couple goals 64

Chapter 10: Grow Together 67
The importance of practicing day after day to achieve a mindful relationship 69
Demystifying the fairytales 71
Arguing in marriages 72

Conclusion 74
SOURCES OF INFORMATION 76
Communication Skills for Couples: 78
Introduction 79

Chapter 1: Skill #1 - Abandoning Your Ego 80
There's No Room for Ego in a Happy Relationship 80
Signs Your Ego Is Damaging Your Relationship 81
Kicking Ego Out the Front Door Once and for All 81

Chapter 2: Skill #2 - How to Build Healthy Habits as A Couple 83
Healthy Habits That Happy Couples Engage In 83

Chapter 3: Skill #3 - Developing Emotional Intelligence 86
Signs That You or Your Partner May Be Lacking Emotional Intelligence 86
How to Work on Bettering Your Emotional Intelligence 87

Chapter 4: Skill #4 - Developing Empathy Listening 89
What Is Empathy Listening? 89
Why Empathy Listening Can Help Communication In a Relationship 89
How to Develop Empathy Listening 90

Chapter 5: Skill #5 - Don't Be Afraid to Show Weakness 92
Why Being Vulnerable Can be a Good Thing for Your Relationship 92
How to Work On Being Less Afraid 92

Chapter 6: Skill #6 – Understanding Body Language 95
Basic Cues to Reading Your Partner's Body Language Correctly 95
How Does Your Partner Behave During an Argument? 97

Chapter 7: Skill #7 – Learning to Talk About It 99
Why You Need to Learn to Talk About It 99
Start Learning How to Talk About It 99

Chapter 8: Skill #8 – Digitally Disconnecting 102
Why We Need to Step Away from Technology 102
How to Disconnect Digitally and Start Being Engaged Physically in Your Relationship 103

Chapter 9: Skill #9 – Apologizing Mindfully 105
The Purpose of an Apology 105
What Happens If You Don't Apologize? 105
Why Some People Find Apologies So Hard? 106
How to Start Apologizing Mindfully 106

Chapter 10: Skill #10 – No Judgment Zone 108
Why Judgment Is Such A Damaging Quality 108
Why Do We Judge the People We Love? 109

How to Stop Judging the People We Love 109

Chapter 11: Skill #11 – Working on Yourself First 111
Where to Begin When It Comes to Self-Improvement 111
Self-Improvement Begins with You 112

Chapter 12: Skill #12 – Using Irony to Diffuse Unpleasant Situations 114
Types of Irony 114
Should We Use Irony in Our Relationships? 115

Chapter 13: Skill 13 – A Couple That Laughs Together, Stays Together 116
How Laughter Can Benefit Your Romantic Relationship 116

Chapter 14: Skill #14 – Don't Neglect the Sexual Aspect 120
Anxiety Over Sexual Relationships 120
How to Recognize the Signs That Your Partner Is Suffering from Sexual Relationship Anxiety 121
What You Can Do to Help Your Partner Through It 121

Chapter 15: Skill #15 – Getting Some Space 123
Why Getting Space Is Important 123

Chapter 16: Skill #16 – Setting Goals Together 126
What Exactly Is a Goal? 126
Why Is It Important to Set Goals as a Couple? 126
How to Start Setting Goals as A Couple 127

Chapter 17: Skill #17 – Don't' Hold onto Anger 129
Why Do We Feel Angry? 129
When Does Anger Become a Problem in A Relationship? 130
How to Start Learning to Let Go 130

Chapter 18: Skill #18 – Sincerity Matters 133
Relationship Happiness Boils Down to Sincerity 133
How to Start Building a Relationship Based on Sincerity 134

Chapter 19: Skill #19 – Productive Conflict Helps 136
Why Productive Conflict Is Good for Your Relationship 136

Chapter 20: Skill #20 – Developing Diplomatic Dialogue Skills 139
What Does Diplomatic Communication Mean? 139
Bringing These Diplomatic Communication Techniques into Your Relationship ... 139

Chapter 21: Skill #21 - Organizing Romantic Meetings 141
Benefits of Romantic Meetings 142

How to Start Planning Romantic Meetings 142

Chapter 22: The 7-Day Challenge - Workshop to Better Communication ..145

Day 1: Reflect and be honest 145

Day 2: Commit to one change.. 145

Day 3: Say 'Hi' like it's a big deal 146

Day 4: Talk about the bad stuff objectively 146

Day 5: Gaze into each other's eyes... 146

Day 6: Compliment your partner and yourself 146

Day 7: Ask questions 146

References: 148

Conclusion 150

Communication for Couples

An Essential Guide: Hear Your Partner to Achieve a Healthy Relationship, Improve Mindful Habits and Grow Empathy for Each Other

INTRODUCTION

Congratulations on downloading the book *Communication for Couples,* and thank you for doing so. The information you find in this book can be put to practice as soon as one wants to. Communication is a task that many people take lightly and assume is easy and does not require much effort. However, one must realize that good communication requires attention and effort, especially for couples.

Downloading this book is the first effort you have made to understanding perfect communication for couples. This first step is the easy part. The information you will find in the following chapters is so crucial that you should take it to heart and apply it in your day to day life. If you do not need the information as at yet, file the tips away and use them when needed. You will be glad that you gathered the information and that you can use the tips.

To that end, the chapters in this book will discuss how empathy is the basis for good communication, empathic listening, the importance of working on yourself first, diplomatic dialogue skills, developing mindful habits, appreciating and accepting your partner for what he or she, the ego monster, loving unconditionally, setting common goals, growing together, and the importance of practicing day after day to achieve a mindful relationship.

There are many books in the market that address the matter of communication for couples, so thank you again for choosing this one. Every effort has been made to make sure that the book delivers valuable and useful information to you. Please enjoy!

CHAPTER 1: WHAT IS EMPATHY?

Empathy refers to the ability to sense the emotions of other people combined with the ability to understand and imagine what they might be feeling or thinking. Not everybody can understand and empathize with other people. Empathy is the basis for good communication.

Some days back, while we were going home from a meeting, we found a homeless woman standing at the corner of the street shaking because of the cold. Her clothes were too thin to protect her from the chilly weather, and she looked weary. In front of her was a signboard that said, "Please help. I will truly appreciate it." As we walked by, most of us stopped to give the woman some dollars. However, one woman, a wife to an acquaintance stood back in disgust and ranted that the homeless people were just lazy. She went ahead to mention that the homeless people were freeloaders who had acquired the skill of offloading people by playing with their emotions. She also dared to say that probably, the homeless woman collected more money from people than her salary. Our male colleague was so embarrassed by the character of his wife until he averted his eyes.

Why is it that some people can feel and understand the suffering of others while others cannot? How is it that some people can remain so cold to others to the extent of being indifferent and uncaring while others can envision the problems, empathize, and even look for ways to help them?

Generally, human beings are well attuned to their own emotions and feelings. As such, people are wired to identify what they and their colleagues are going through. However, it requires empathy for us to be able to walk in the shoes of other people and helping them so to speak. Empathy supports the human ability to understand the emotions and feeling the other person is experiencing. For many people, it is easy to respond with kindness and gentleness to people who are undergoing challenges and as such, showing hostility to an already troubled person is incomprehensible. However, like in the case mentioned earlier scenario, it is not everyone who can empathize with other people; we can, therefore, say that empathy is not a thing that applies to all people all the time.

So, what does empathy entail? In the year 1909, psychologist Edward B. Titchener introduces the term empathy from the German word 'einfühlung.' The word 'einfühlung' can be defined as 'feeling into.' It refers to the ability to emotionally and psychologically understand the experiences of another person. Mostly, one gets to the position of the other person and somehow feels what they must be going through. The word empathy is used to refer to a variety of experiences depending on the context. For instance, Emotional researchers define the term as the ability to imagine the thoughts and feelings of another combined with the ability to sense the emotions involved.

On the other hand, contemporary researchers look at empathy from 2 angles; Affective empathy and cognitive empathy. Affective empathy refers to the feelings and sensations that one gets in response to the emotions of the other person. It may involve feeling stressed and anxious because someone else is suffering. Cognitive empathy is the ability to understand and identify the feelings of other people. Scientists have found that some experiences, conditions, and disorders make it hard for some people to empathize.

Empathy has been found to have some deep roots in the brains and bodies of human beings and other animals. Many studies in neuroscience suggest that empathy is found in both human beings and animals. It can be linked to a majority of mammals. For instance, dolphins have been seen to save humans and other creatures from drowning or being eaten by sharks. Animals as big as an elephant have shown most of the characteristics of empathy and compassion towards each other and also to other creatures. Behavior studies of the primates in the wild as well as in captivity have indicated that they are empathic and more so the Bonobos.

Closer to home, the dogs have shown elements of empathy and so have rats. Remember that having empathy does not necessarily mean that one wants to help the people in trouble although this is usually the first vital step towards compassionate actions. The empathy experience normally facilitates the pro-social behavior of the ability to help others without being forced. Empathy promotes a level of compassion that is different for every individual. Most people desire to be listened to with compassion and understanding, and they want the listener to feel beyond the words. Empathy demonstrates care to such people.

In most cases, empathy is an excellent thing when applied well. It increases positivity, principles and high ethical standards. However, some people say that too much empathy interferes with the rational thinking capacity of an individual. Too much empathy may have detrimental effects on the individual and the world at large. When people lead too much with the heart rather than the head, they tend to lose the big picture, and they feel the long term consequences of over empathy.

We should note that empathizing with another person does not mean that the emotional state of the empath matches the other person in every detail. Rather, empathy implies that we share and understand the feelings, experiences, and emotions of the other person using our mind to simulate the scenes based on our past experiences. For example, if someone is ill, we understand their pain by associating their experience to our past events of sickness.

Given that human beings use their feelings and experiences as the model for sharing and understanding the experiences of other people, some researchers say that empaths engage both emotional and the cognitive process in feeling and thinking about the experience of the other person. Scientific studies show that in many cases, the medial prefrontal cortex shows robust activation as soon as we think (cognitively) about the feelings and emotions of other people. However, the studies also show that the central regions of the same prefrontal cortex show superior activation of the emotion-angle taking tasks compared to the cognitive perspective. This analysis of the brain suggests that the ventral part may be involved more in affective (feeling) processing while the dorsal region handles the more challenging task of cognitive (thinking) processing.

We can, therefore, say that once a person starts empathizing with someone, he/she uses the cognitive processes to try and analyze the emotional state. Next, the person imagines himself/herself in a particular state by drawing on the emotional memories he/she had in the past. Ultimately, the person embodies the emotions he/she is imagining. As we try to understand how the seemingly complex process of empathy develops and why it is that people and even other animals are emotionally affected by the experiences of others, scientists have identified two potential precursors namely, imitation and emotional contagion. Imitation refers to the establishment of correspondence between the behavior one person and another. For instance, newborn babies will tend to copy their parents in an effortful and consistent way beginning with simple acts like sticking out a tongue. Imitation does not force one to change the emotional state, but it gives one the opportunity to learn how and when certain feelings occur. From imitation, people become better at processing the feelings of others.

On the other hand, emotional contagion is defined as the tendency to directly or indirectly catch the emotions of the other person. For instance, a baby might start crying just because he/she has had another one cry. These contagions can occur unconsciously and outside our awareness. We cannot say that imitation and emotional contagion are the only precursors of empathy, but it is evident that behavioral and biological mechanisms underlying the two aspects overlap with the process of empathy. We can also say that empathy, imitation, and emotional contagion contributes to pro-social behavior. All three constructs are found in human beings and many animals, but empathy is more evident in people than animals because it requires higher degrees of emotional and cognitive processing.

Summarily, empathy is the bedrock of close connection and intimacy. If we did not have empathy, relationships would be so emotionally shallow that shared activities and mutual interests would be the only common aspects between people. Again, if human beings did not have empathy, they would work together but never really understand the feelings of each other and even the inner selves. Life would be like being in a subway with total strangers who have no idea what the other person is about. Empathy does not only fuel pro-social behavior and closeness, but also, it helps people to stop when they act up because of the awareness of the pain and bad emotions they might be causing. Empathy puts breaks on excessive self-interest; otherwise, we would have scorched earth. Please note that empathy and sympathy do not have a similar meaning.

CHAPTER 2: EMPATHIC LISTENING (USING EMPATHY TO LISTEN TO YOUR PARTNER)

Psychologists have found that human beings are wired for empathy by the deep attachment relationships developed in the two early years of life. Studies have revealed that 18-month-olds are able to put themselves in the shoes of someone else to some extent. This empathy does not stop developing once people have grown up; rather, people nurture its growth throughout life. As such, empathy becomes a radical force supporting social transformation.

Different people have different levels of empathy and scholars have classified them accordingly. For example, there are people who have a complete lack of empathy. Such people find it very hard to maintain relationships and have no contact with remorse. They cannot understand how another person is feeling, and they may or may not be cruel. Some of the people identified under this category include narcissistic individuals, psychopaths, and borderline personalities.

Other categories of empaths include (1) those who have empathy but lack self-control such that they easily hurt people when they are upset, (2) those who have difficulties with empathy but they have enough empathy to understand the impact of their actions after they have hurt someone, and (3) those who have a difficult time showing and having empathy because they know they do not see things as other people do and are never quite normal. Normal men tend to have low amounts of empathy, and in most cases, they avoid talking about emotions and as such, they base friendships on shared activities. Women, on the other hand, tend to have an above average level of empathy and they apply care when dealing with other people and stay sensitive to their feelings.

Have you ever realized how some people make you feel understood and validated without saying anything? What is the secret about them that makes it so simple for you to 'open up' and share your problems? Why are they the first person you go to whenever you want to unburden your soul? The answer to this question is simple – empathic listening.

That is what makes them the ideal conversation partners. It's the reason why everyone else seems to gravitate around them. It's why they get along well with everyone in the office and can click almost instantly with every person they meet.

In case you didn't know, empathic listening is an ability which means it can be learned through practice and repetition. And that's precisely what you're going to get out of this article.

Empathy: the cornerstone of authentic human interactions
In a world where time is a scarce resource and everyone seems to be running after something, it has become increasingly difficult for many of us to exercise patience and listen to others, before we express our own opinions and desires.

We expect others to understand us without ever putting ourselves in their shoes. We want others to resonate with our views without giving them a chance to voice their opinions. And even if they do express their views or offer some constructive criticism, we rarely return the favor.

As a result, our day-to-day interactions can become nothing more than a 'cold' exchange of replies; no 'real' connection, no empathy. But it doesn't have to be that way. If you are willing to listen instead of talk, understand instead of criticizing, and comfort instead of judging, you can quickly turn a conversation into an authentic human interaction.

Whether you're talking to your spouse, friend, boss, coworker, neighbor or even the barista who works at your favorite coffee shop, empathic listening can significantly improve the quality of your interaction. Contrary to popular belief, it was collaboration, not competition that helped humankind survive, thrive, and reach the level of socio-economic development we see today. And one of the keys to an authentic and fruitful collaboration is empathic listening.

What is empathic listening?
In a nutshell, empathic listening means to hear your conversation partner authentically. It's the ability to listen with the sincere intention of understanding other people's values, opinions, and ideas.

Empathic listening allows you to get 'in tune with their frequency' and resonate on an emotional level. It means to get in touch with their needs and make them feel heard.

Empathic listening opens a window to their inner universe and creates a safe space where they can share anything without having to worry about criticism or bad remarks.

When empathy is the bridge that brings two people together, words become less important and what matters most is the connection between them.

But being empathetic does not mean you have to agree with everything and does not imply any obligation on your part. It only involves an effort to understand other people's perspective; 'to walk a mile in their shoes' so to speak.

Sadly, not all people are naturally born with empathy; not everyone finds it easy to identify, process, and resonate with other people's emotions. However, we can develop and sharpen this skill through patience and exercise. Those of us who are disconnected from our feelings will find it a bit difficult, but not impossible to learn to improve empathy. Just as any other ability, empathic listening can be acquired, as long as you're motivated and willing to take it stepwise and practice consistently.

How does empathic listening relate to happiness?
Some of you may be wondering how exactly does listening to others and trying to resonate emotionally with them contribute to our well-being. What does empathic listening have to do with happiness?

First of all, empathetic ears are hard to come by these days. Many people are too self-involved to care about what others have to say. But given that healthy social interactions are critical to our growth, knowing how empathize is one of the ingredients of a happy and fulfilling life.

Second, research suggests that when you listen in an empathic manner, people are satisfied with the conversation and you instantly become more socially attractive. And since we're all social creatures by nature, being able to navigate social situations successfully will indirectly contribute to our overall sense of happiness and well-being.

Finally, given that empathic listeners are social magnets, they often benefit from exciting opportunities that contribute to their personal and professional growth. Overall, empathic listening can significantly add to our overall sense of happiness and well-being. Perhaps this is the secret to lasting joy and whole fulfilling life.

Empathic listening for couples
Empathic communication is an essential component of any successful and lasting relationship. The ability to be empathetic towards your loved one has significant effects on the overall level of satisfaction you and your partner experience in your relationship.

As you can imagine, knowing how to listen with an open mind - without interruptions, criticism, and unwanted advice – is a 'must' in any healthy and functional couple.

Too often, people who love each other end up splitting because of communication issues. Whether it manifests as stonewalling, criticism, or contempt, lack of empathy can slowly turn two people into two strangers who resent each other.

And that's because one of our fundamental needs is to be heard and understood. When this does not happen, you begin to feel lonely and abandoned. You suffer and eventually distance yourself, even from a person you loved more than you could ever imagine.

Experts suggest empathic listening paves the way for affectionate communication, a crucial element for any healthy couple. When empathic listening becomes a habit that characterizes your relationship, you can easily resonate with your partner's struggles and understand why he/she might be feeling that way. And this gives you the chance to find solutions and fix the 'cracks' that could compromise your relationship.

All and all, empathic listening builds strong relationships, fosters effective communications, and cultivates trust between life partners.

Empathic listening at work
In a way, we could argue that empathic listening is a 21st-century skill.

That means we not only use it to achieve personal growth by cultivating a thriving social life and building lasting romantic relationships, but also to advance in our career by investing in fruitful partnerships.

From leadership and business to sales and negotiation, empathy seems to be one of those variables that can tip the scale in your favor, overcome 'formal' barriers, and appeal to people's 'soft' side.

Empathic listening plays such an important role in activities like sales that researchers have even begun developing tools to measure it. One example is the active empathic listening (AEL) scale which evaluates three dimensions: sensing, processing, and responding. More specifically, this scale assesses how well the person can zero-in on emotions, process them, and come up with an appropriate answer.

If you wish to become a better boss, leader, coworker or even employee, empathic listening should be among your 'sharpest' skills. Just because you talk to your boss, client, business partner, or coworker doesn't mean you should keep the conversation at a formal level. Appeal to their emotions, make them feel understood, and you will be on the right path towards a productive partnership.

In time, empathic listening can set the stage for fantastic business opportunities which directly contribute to a happy and prosperous life.

How to practice empathic listening?

Since developing empathic listening is all about practice, let's focus on a brief example that will show you how proper empathic communication should look like.

Mary: So, what's new in your life?

James: Hmm, nothing much.

Mary: You seem a bit off. Is everything ok? **(She detects a negative emotional vibe and uses a question to dig deeper)**

James: Just some minor problems with Mary; nothing so important.

Mary: You want to talk about it? I'm here for you. Maybe I can help you out in some way. **(She makes herself available and lets him know he can rely on her)**

James: I don't remember, things haven't been right between us lately.

Mary: I'm sorry to hear that. I don't want to be too nosy, but did something happen between you two? **(She asks open-ended questions but without being intrusive)**

James: Well, I don't know if I should burden you with my problems.

Mary: It's ok. Don't worry. If you feel like sharing, I'm here for you **(She creates a safe space)**

James: Hmmm, things kind of went south about a month ago when I noticed she was texting with a guy from work. Although she told me there's nothing between them and I should stop making a big deal out of it, I can't help but think she might be having an affair with this guy.

Mary: So, because she's texting with this guy from work, you're worried it might be more between them? **(She paraphrases to make sure she got the message right and make him feel understood)**

James: Yes. And I know it sounds crazy, but I can't get this idea out of my head. God, I'm such a mess! I love her so much, but I'm afraid I'm going to lose her because of my stupid jealousy.

Mary: Look, James, I know you love Mary, and I know you don't want to lose her. Maybe that's why you're acting so jealous. **(She paraphrases his message, empathizes with him)**

Mary: But are there any other reasons you think she might be cheating on you? **(She asks open-ended questions to understand the situation further)**

James: Well, no. I don't think so. Maybe this whole cheating thing is just in my head.

Mary: Want some advice? **(She asks before giving advice)**

James: Sure.

Mary: Talk to your girl. Tell her what you told me. Tell her that you're acting this way because you love her and don't want to lose her. **(She encourages him to have a conversation with his girlfriend and clarify the situation)**

James: What if she doesn't understand? What if she thinks I'm crazy?

Mary: Then maybe you two could see a couple's counselor. Who knows? It might be the solution you need to fix this issue. **(She offers an alternative solution)**

James: I guess that could be an option. Thanks, Mary; it was constructive talking to you.

Mary: My pleasure! And thanks for placing your trust in me. If you ever need an empathetic ear, I'm here for you. **(She validates his confidence and extends her support)**

9 strategies to develop empathic listening

1. it's not about you

Whenever you're talking to someone and wish to lend an empathetic ear, the first thing you need to understand is that it's not about you.

That's the secret to authentic empathic listening – placing your conversation partner above your needs.

And it can be quite hard to put aside personal opinions and make it all about him/her. After all, you're not his/her therapist.

So, before you decide to be there for someone, make sure you're available emotionally. Otherwise, there's no point in encouraging him or her to share a personal issue for which you're not ready to provide understanding and support.

2. Put away your phone

Too often we find ourselves checking our phone or answering a text message while the other person may be pouring their heart out.

This is one of those unpleasant habits that many of us have adopted as a result of living in the digital era. We get so hooked on social media that we sometimes end up losing sight of the person who's right there in front of us.

And it's impossible to establish an emotional bond when you're regularly checking your phone, and all you can say is *"Aha"* or *"I understand."* So, whenever you wish to offer empathy and create an authentic connection put your phone away and asks the other person to do the same.

3. Be an active listener

In a way empathic listening and active listening are synonymous. Being an active listener means being present in the conversation. It means ignoring any distractions and focusing exclusively on the person in front of you.

Active listeners live in the 'here and now.' They immerse themselves into the other person's universe and seek to gain a better understanding of the topic in discussion.

Of course, that doesn't mean you have to listen and nod in silence. A conversation is a two-way street where both partners exchange ideas, impressions, and seek to resonate with one another emotionally.

In short, active listening is about presence and depth.

4. Refrain from criticism

As you can probably imagine, empathic listening implies a high degree of emotional intelligence. When someone shares a story or event that holds significance to him/her, it would be ideal to refrain from evaluations, criticism, or negative feedback.

There are times when other people's problems may seem trivial, ridiculous, or even infuriating. But once again, it's not about you, it about them. Remember, your goal is to understand and provide emotional support. Any form of criticism will only create tension and make it difficult for you to 'forge' authentic connections. Listen, understand, and empathize.

5. Adjust your body language

As you probably know, body language is of paramount importance for genuine social interactions. When it comes to empathic listening, your body can help you create the kind of communication that makes room for understanding and empathy.

Your posture and gestures can either bring people closer or create a barrier that makes it difficult for you to listen actively and empathically.

If you want to make people feel safe and welcome, make sure to adopt a relaxed posture with open arms and constant eye contact. You can even go for a friendly pat on the shoulder or even a warm hug.

6. Paraphrase your conversation partner

Paraphrasing is among the most effective strategies for empathic listening. Letting your conversation partner know that you understand his perspective creates an ideal climate for sharing emotions.

Many studies suggest that paraphrasing – along with clarifying, questioning, and remembering details – are the critical elements of empathic listening. Furthermore, this creates a safe space where people can share and engage in self-exploration. Paraphrasing your conversation partner is relatively easy. All you need to do is listening to what your partner has to say and rephrase his/her message.

7. Ask open-ended questions

If you want your conversation partner to share, you need to 'fuel' the conversation by asking open questions. Sometimes, people don't 'open up' that easily. Not everyone will be willing to talk to you openly, especially when it comes to personal problems. And that's why you need to give him or her a push by using questions that create opportunities for sharing.

Although smart questions can enrich a conversation, make sure you're not intrusive. You're supposed to have a happy talk, not an interview.

If you notice that your partner doesn't feel comfortable, refrain from asking questions and let him or her dictate the flow of the conversation.

8. Stop giving unsolicited advice

When you're looking to establish an emotional connection with someone, the worst thing you can do is offer unsolicited advice. Nothing 'kills' the vibe of a good conversation more than telling the other person what he or she should do. Remember that empathic listening is mostly about understanding and 'connectedness.' Sometimes, all it takes to establish an emotional connection is active listening.

If, however, you think you have a good piece of advice to offer, ask your conversation partner if he/she is interested in hearing it.

9. Don't 'fill up' the silence

Many of us tend to feel awkward during the occasional moments of silence that are specific to any conversation. But silence can be a powerful tool in establishing an authentic connection is you know how to use it. You can use silence to allow the other person to take charge of the conversation or give him/her enough time to process your input and come up with an answer.

And let's not forget that a conversation doesn't rely solely on a constant exchange of words. There's also your body language which through which you can express empathy and build an authentic connection.

The importance of empathic listening

Empathic listening is also called reflective listening or active listening. It is a way of listening and responding to others that enhances trust and mutual understanding. It is a vital skill for disputants and third parties as well because it makes it possible for the listener to accurately interpret the received message from the speaker and provide a relevant response. The response is a fundamental part of the process of listening and can be essential to the success of mediation or negotiation. Empathic listening has numerous benefits that include:

- It will build respect and trust
- Enables the conflicting parties to release their emotions
- It will reduce your tension
- It will create a safe and conducive environment for collaborative solving of problems
- It will encourage the surfacing of essential details

Strategies to develop empathetic listening
- It is not about you
- Put away your phone
- Be an active listener
- Refrain from criticism
- Adjust your body language
- Ask open-ended questions
- Paraphrase your conversation when talking to your partner

In summary:
All in all, empathic listening represents the foundation of effective communication and one of the secrets to lasting relationships.

When you're willing to put aside your personal views and seek to empathize with others, people will gravitate around you. That, in turn, will result in authentic relationships and fruitful business partnerships. Even if you are not a natural born empathy, you can still develop this skill as long as you're willing to:

- Make the conversation about the person in front of you
- Avoid distractions
- Listen actively and refrain from criticism or advice-giving
- Paraphrase and ask open-ended questions
- Adjust your body language
- Use silence to your advantage.

Listen empathically, and others will be drawn naturally to your social circle.

CHAPTER 3: THE IMPORTANCE OF WORK ON YOURSELF FIRST

The couple is made of two people; both must be responsible for their balance first. Change yourself to the better if you want to help your partner to be a better person.
Everybody gets angry for one reason or the other. Whether it shows or not, we are all bound to feeling tension when people overstep their boundaries, or certain matters go wrong. In marriages, spouses can avoid showing anger to avoid conflict. They shove it down and let it go unnoticed.

However, hidden anger is just as bad as that which explodes because, at one point or the other, it will hurt the relationship. In most cases, the more one lets the arguments to go on, the more the distance between him/her and the partner grows. The longer it lasts, the harder it is for the couple to repair the relationship and at such points, people look for divorce papers.

As human beings, anger pushes us to say or do things that WE would not do in normal circumstances. We should remember that once words are said and actions are done, it is impossible to unsay or undo them. When we explode, we should be careful about how we deal with anger. The emotion of anger is not right or wrong by itself. The morality of emotions and feelings comes in question only when we react to what we are feeling. For example, feeling angry is okay but destroying things out of anger brings the morality aspect.

Causes of conflicts between couples
More often than not, human beings forget that they are different and that each has a different opinion and view of things. This happens a lot in marriage because the love and attraction make the couple feel like they are one. Although marriage brings 'two people together to become one' their minds still differ, their backgrounds are different, their upbringing is different; therefore they cannot have the same opinions all the time.

Everyone has a different memory and perception, and there is no one right and standard way of thinking. Even when you know that your opinion is right, your line of thought and perspective is not the only right one. A couple consists of two people, and if it is only one person who keeps giving their opinion without considering the opinion of the other one, then the marriage is made up on one person. This means that there is no room in the marriage for the two people and thus the communication stops, and the marriage no longer functions properly.

There are many different ways of dealing with issues positively without having fights that will end up destroying the communication. Spouses do not have to strive to fix each other rather; they should look for ways to agree and disagree positively. A couple should constantly deal with unresolved anger and issues. Do not bottle up things, feelings, emotions, opinions et cetera even if it is for the sake of the other person. Letting thing go without sorting them out fast and soon only leads to deeper conflicts and more distance to the extent of everyone using a confrontational tone and attitude even when they should not.

How to deal with anger
Firstly, when a spouse is wrong, he/she should not hesitate to apologize. Words such as 'I am sorry' go a long way in making a partner reconsider their next words. When honesty is applied by the person apologizing, there is no more room for more arguments. Conceding defeat does not make one weak and apologizing helps to loosen tension which might have escalated to disconnection and complete lack of communication. Staying stubborn and trying to 'fix' a partner will not help solve anything. Standing a ground is only necessary when the couple will win together but if the victory belongs to one person, chances are a brick wall will grow between them. It is therefore important that everybody communicates effectively, practice saying the right things to each other, build one another, talk to each other and avoid talking at one another.

Communication as a cornerstone to work on yourself
If one were to go to a crowd of people and ask them to name the most important aspect of marriage, they would mention a variety of things including trust, honesty love et cetera. Every person has their understanding of love and marriage, and they have their preferences. Of course, all the aspects that the people would mention play a crucial role in marriages but communication is the centerpiece of all communication.

The way the two spouses communicate with each other, discuss their issues, encourage and build one another through communication is essential for the sustainment of a fulfilling marriage. One can say that communication is the vehicle that carries all the other aspects of marriage. Without communication, that is verbal and verbal; a spouse could not know whether to trust and be honest with their partners. Assumptions usually break the marriage. If one person loves the other and does not talk about it or at least show it in words, they will not succeed in marriage. To the spouses; if you love your partner, let them know through words and actions.

If the communication between two people is honest, then the chances of the relationship surviving are high. Communication is the cornerstone of all relationship; however, many people are not good at communicating. Other people do not know how to address matters in the right way. Spouses need to use certain communication channels to create a strong and caring atmosphere in their marriage. Love, honesty trust and other important parts of marriage are not meaningful by themselves. One must be able to express these aspects to give them meaning. The expression of love and care in marriage is what makes it worth envy. Showing love acting honestly and showcasing trust is where the magic of marriage lies. The ability to communicate with a spouse about how much they mean to each other is where a marriage graduates from good to great. One should remember that communication is more than speaking about things; it is also showing. Under the umbrella of communication between couples, we can identify verbal, non-verbal and physical acts.

Verbal communication between couples

Verbal communication is the easiest and most commonly used form of communication. Words are easy to use to a large extent. People like to hear things especially when they are nice. For instance, every spouse loves to be complemented through words 'you look very nice today,' 'I love you.' You are a great person with an amazing personality.' Effective communication requires one to be able to express their feelings to their spouse through words. If a couple loves each other so much yet they are unable to communicate the same through words; they might never know how much they mean to each other. Even when the actions show clearly that the spouses love one another, they still need to say it in words. Words will add value to the actions and vice versa. They will make the involved parties feel appreciated, loved, and sure about how the other person feels.

Along with all the compliments and expression of the positive, the spouses can express what they are not happy about through words. If a spouse is doing something that is offending the other, yet the offended person is silent about it, the offender will most probably continue with their habits. Silence does not help in most cases. If anything, lack of communication will keep hurting the couple. One cannot possibly go through life while holding all the dissatisfaction inside. Verbal communication will help one let it all out. However, when letting matters out, one should be tactful and careful. Care and warmth in communication are essential, especially when talking about matters that might bring disagreements. Couples should not wait too long before they say something about things bothering them. They should also not wait too long before telling each other that they care.

Nonverbal communication between couples

At some point in life, we have said something unpleasant or unfriendly to someone else. They might not have retaliated verbally, but they show their displeasure through facial expressions and actions either voluntarily or involuntarily. The offended person did not have to say a word to tell the story, but it all showed on their faces. Human beings share more with their faces and body than they would give credit.

Spouses should be aware of their facial expression and body language while talking to their partners to avoid giving off the wrong message. Human beings are capable of reading the body language of their partners even subconsciously. If for example, a couple is having a serious conversation and one person id hunched over and probably closed off, the other will detect a lack of vulnerability. Use the right facial and body language for every conversation. For example, if a couple s having a serious conversation, it is important that the two parties Face each other and keep their body language open without crossing the legs or arms. The body language should show that the person is listening keenly, taking note of the important things and is willing to work through the subject matter. Nonverbal cues are many, and they communicate to the partner either positively or negatively even without an exchange of words. Everyone should be conscious and thoughtful of how their body language brings out their thoughts.

Physical acts

Physical acts include making dinner, doing the laundry, taking out the garbage, and even getting ice-cream from the fridge for a pregnant wife. Physical actions are not things one can express through words. They are things that one does for their spouses to show them how much they care. IN DOING SUCH simple things, one is communicating with their partners about how much they mean to them without using words. This form of communication falls under the phrase "Actions speak louder than words." You could sing your spouse that you love them till your face turns blue, but it would not mean as much as making him/her dinner or replacing their old attire. The power of actions outdoes the power of saying I love you 300 times a day.

Having in mind that communication is important for the success of marriage; one cannot rely on just one of the ways mentioned above. Every spouse should strike a balance between the three to ensure that the marriage thrives. It is okay for a spouse to tell their partner that they love them and at the same time give an opinion about things that are bothering them. Open communication will benefit the marriage in the long term and become an investment to reap from. Every person should use body language to show their spouses that they are honest and open with them. An observant eye will pick negative body language no matter how well one hides it. A spouse may take this as a red flag for the beginning of the end of the marriage. Couples need to stay alert about what they communicate through their bodies and make appropriate adjustments so that the spouse can read honesty and trust

Again, a couple should use actions to communicate to their spouses A gift or two, a body massage, a dinner date, or even assisting with a troubling task can go a long way to communicate to each other. Actions will always speak for themselves; even if one was to keep singing that they love someone yet they fail to show it in actions, then they will fail. Without open and effective communication, a couple will face more challenges and obstacles than otherwise.

CHAPTER 4: DIPLOMATIC DIALOGUE SKILLS

Diplomatic dialogue skills are a better way to talk while respecting your partner sensibility.

Is there one thing that can be defined as the key to a good marriage? It is hard to answer this question in one word. Every marriage is different; the couples have different things that keep them and their relationship successful. Whether the couple is newly wedded or it is the 'Ball and chain' marriage that has lasted for years, all people have their share of highs and lows. This may sound cliché, but every marriage has patterns and lulls of mundanity which are as important as the highs.

The good and the bad are natural to the flow and ebb of life. Periods of boredom, stress, poor c communication, and misunderstandings are all part of the course. And it is true to say 'Marriage takes work and commitment.' Every spouse has to work to make the marriage a beautiful place to be. However, the work done in marriages is not like cleaning trash and getting complete makeovers. The effort that couples put into successful marriages (functional happy and fulfilling relationships) is therapeutic and fulfilling.

What's the secret to a long and happy marriage? It's not grand romantic gestures. The trick is establishing healthy habits and doing those little things day after day, year after year. I asked relationship therapists what the happiest couples say or do that gives the relationship the power to stay. Here is what they told me:

- **They make a point to connect every day**

Couples who are in it for the long haul find little ways to stay physically and emotionally connected, even on the busy days. That might mean going in for a gentle, long hug, listening attentively while your partner is venting (not looking at your phone, *ahem*) or offering words of affirmation and encouragement.

"Emotional connection is the glue in our relationships," marriage and family therapist Jennifer Chappell Marsh told HuffPost. "Over time, these small interactions build into a deep sense of trust and intimacy that keep couples happy and together."

- **They set aside time to check in with each other regularly**

When life gets hectic, couples often switch into autopilot and start going through the motions rather than being intentional about nurturing the relationship. Long-lasting couples, however, make it a point to regularly schedule opportunities to stop, slow down and check in with each other. It might be a quick nightly catch-up session before bed or a more in-depth yearly sit-down conversation.

"Planned check-ins are times when both are mentally prepared to provide each other the space they need to explore, resolve and plan," marriage and family therapist Spencer Northey said. "One couple I know even has an annual 'State of the Union Conference,' where they rent a hotel room and have a 'conference' at the hotel bar to check in and make plans for the coming year."

- **They know how to say sorry and mean it**

"In big or small ways, partners step on each other's toes all the time," said psychologist Ryan Howes. "Having the humility and maturity to recognize your role in your partner's pain is essential for a long-term relationship."

And, for the record: "Sorry your feelings were hurt" is a half-assed attempt. Instead, aim for an apology that expresses empathy for your partner, takes responsibility for your wrongdoings and shows that you're working to change the behavior.

Howes' suggested that "I see that you're hurt, and it kills me to see you in this pain. I take full responsibility for my part in this, and I'm taking these steps to make sure it doesn't happen again."

- **And they don't hold on to grudges**

Mistakes will be made. Fights will be had. It's par for the course in any relationship. But couples who go the distance don't hold grudges and let resentments fester. They discuss it, work through it and move forward.

"They understand that mistakes are lessons learned and not reasons to shame or punish each other," psychologist and sex therapist Janet Brito said. "When mistakes occur, they are certain that they are still loved and valued."

Spouses who don't hold past transgressions over the other's head are better equipped to handle future conflicts maturely, Howes said.

"Some folks seem to be grievance collectors, who hold on to every relational sin from their partner and wheel them out for the big arguments, especially if they're losing," he said. "'You forgot my birthday 17 years ago' or 'you made me pay for our third date' are grabs at power and rarely result in a constructive conversation. The healthiest couples express how they feel if and when they've been hurt, they do what they can to make sure it doesn't reoccur, they accept the apology, and then they work hard to let go and live in the present."

- **They find little ways to show they are thinking of each other**

Take some time to remind your partner why you love and appreciate them. Longtime couples are in the habit of regularly expressing how much they mean to each other. It doesn't need to be some vast, romantic overture either. It might mean shooting them a text during the workday to thank them for packing you a tasty lunch or picking up a bottle of the wine they were raving about on your honeymoon.

"It could be something you saw that reminded you of them, or you remembered a shared experience that made you smile and wanted to let them know," therapist Juan Olmedo said. "The key is that it be spontaneous: Even an unexpected text message can brighten their day. And no reciprocation is needed. It's just about telling them that you were thinking about them."

- **They communicate about the fun stuff *and* the not-so-fun stuff**

Talking about the positive things in your life — an exciting job offer, the trip you're planning with your best friends — is easy. Talking about the less glamorous — your crippling anxiety disorder, the dissatisfaction you're feeling in your sex life — can be decidedly less fun but essential nevertheless. It's often these more robust conversations that bring you two closer.

"Couples who stay together have uncomfortable conversations where they share difficult emotions," Chappell Marsh said. "When couples feel their expression of distress is seen and heard, their bond strengthens, they become more resilient and their capacity for overall happiness increases."

- **They accept each other's friends and family, imperfections and all**

Maybe your husband's high school buddy is a significant story-topper, and it gets on your nerves. Or perhaps it irks you that your mother-in-law pulls you aside at every family gathering to ask if you're pregnant yet. Even the happiest couples occasionally get annoyed with their partner's friends and family. It's unavoidable. But these couples also recognize that if the person is vital to their partner, it's probably best to smile and suck it up. (Note that the grin-and-bear-it approach may not be appropriate if the friend or relative in question is a toxic person.)

"They make efforts to get to know the most important people in each other's lives," Brito said. "Instead of criticizing each other's loved ones, they focus on their strengths and similarities, and find ways to cultivate a bond, especially if this is important to their partner."

- **In a healthy and happy relationship, couples talk openly and freely**

They understand that their information and message is safe and well receipted. In the initial stages of a relationship, couples can talk about almost everything without worrying about being judged or misinterpreted. Ones they settle in a marriage, communication becomes tougher as the spouses seek to communicate in a respectful yet fun way. Couples in good relationships are comfortable when voicing their worries showing their feelings when problems arise and also express gratitude when things work out. Open and good relationships involve people who talk respectfully to one another without using the accusatory tone with hurtful and insulting things. Everyone listens attentively and ensures that they understand the message that the other person is putting across, verbally and non-verbally. Couples that apply good communication skills show empathy and do not interrupt the other person while trying to prove that the opinions are wrong. At the end of a good conversation, every person feels that their needs have been acknowledged and understood. Good conversations lead to positivity.

- **They make an effort to understand their partner's perspective, even when they don't agree**

Listening to your partner is essential in any relationship, but it's only half the battle. Long-lasting couples hear each other out and then show that they genuinely understand the other's point of view.

"We all have a fundamental need for understanding, so it's crucial to find ways to tell your partner that you understand what she or he is trying to convey, even if you don't agree," Olmedo said. "Being able to say, 'I get what you're saying,' or 'I can see why that matters to you,' can set the stage for you to get your chance to feel heard. Being genuine here is critical."

- **They celebrate their differences, not just their similarities**

At the beginning of a relationship, it may seem like you and your partner have so much in common: You're both introverts who love hiking on the weekends, chowing down on Korean barbecue and watching Pixar movies. But as time wears on, it becomes clear that, although you may be similar in some ways, you're not the same person. Longtime couples can recognize that these differences keep things interesting and help you both grow.

"Some couples have the unrealistic expectation that they'll enjoy all the same hobbies, have the same opinions and beliefs, and react to life with the same emotions. When they don't, they can feel alone or even abandoned," Howes said. "The healthiest couples can appreciate their partner's different tastes and responses and react to them with curiosity instead of scorn. 'What? Do you like that candidate? I'm so curious why that is because I have exactly the opposite reaction. Tell me more.'"

- **They don't make assumptions about their partner's feelings — they ask**

In the heat of an argument, it's easy to jump to conclusions about what your partner is thinking or feeling. But successful longtime couples can focus on the context of the disagreement at hand, instead of making sweeping generalizations.

"Instead of making broad conclusions about a situation, they inquire about the circumstances and setting, to consider all angles," Brito said. "They don't assume what the other person is feeling but are curious to inquire and are prepared to listen without judgment."

Often, couples who don't know how to argue terminate their arguments prematurely because they're too frustrated or heated to resolve them appropriately. But if you don't come to some resolution — even a temporary one — how can you ever move forward?

"Even though arguments are challenging, you've got to stick with it to find the compromise or solution that you both can live with," Howes said. "I've known couples who never seem to get to the point of resolution with their arguments, and this has a toxic effect on the relationship.

A survey conducted on couples in marriages that had lasted for more than 15 years revealed different basic tips that ensured their success. Below are six tips that were common in almost all the couples:

- **Independence**

One of the aspects that the couples rated as really important for the success of the marriage were Independence. Everyone must first have their happiness before seeking happiness in a relationship. Having that in mind, every spouse must take time by themselves, enjoy their hobbies, and pursue their desires. Spend some time apart; it will help everyone reestablish their sense of self and check their progress. You should remember that absence makes the heart grow fonder. Too much dependency makes one unable to move forward. Independence will keep the conversation fresh in the marriage, and everyone will be more attractive to their partner.

- **Good listening**

Every spouse should work on their listening skills. Men tend to complain that women are annoying because they talk too much and in some cases, the talk is not constructive. They fail to realize that for many women, all that matters is a listening ear. Men need to listen to women and women too need to work on active listening. One should remember that hearing and listening differ. Hearing involves the years while listening entails the heart. Before any person talks, they should listen. Listen and listen some more.

- **Agree to disagree**

Being in a good relationship does not mean that everybody agrees on everything. Many of the couples revealed that they have different attitudes, belief systems, and opinions. They have opposing opinions on some major areas of life. Every couple should have a level of disagreement to maintain balance. As such, every loving couple should agree to disagree and even seek the sense of humor their point of disagreement.

- **Communicate**

In marriage, communication involves identifying the love language of each other. Every individual has a different way of communicating love to their spouse. When one understands the hobbies and preferences of their partner, they will understand the metaphors they use to communicate love. Some people prefer to show rather than speak love. Others prefer to show it by doing favors such as making dinner, picking the children from school, et cetera. Some people prefer to write letters and leave notes for their partners while others prefer physical affection. Couples fail to pay much attention to the language of love thinking that it is a small matter; however, understanding love language is essential.

- **Acceptance**

Acceptance is essential for the success of a marriage. Lack of acceptance is often attributed to spouses who nag. Every spouse should remember that he or she married their partner for who he/she was then and who they are now. Even if the partners change, we should accept them for who they are before we even try to change them. Couples should not focus their arguments on the weaknesses of each other, and when one wishes to correct the other, they should apply tactfulness. Spouses should complement each other and acknowledge their positive attributes daily. This will encourage everybody to stay on the positive side and increase acceptance.

- **Never take each other for granted**

When couples get comfortable in marriage, they tend to take each other for granted. This is one of the most toxic pathogens in marriage. Getting comfortable makes people forget important things including communication. It is human to get comfortable with what they know, but in marriage, couples should not be in a state where they take each other for granted. Every spouse should pledge to respect their partner no matter what. Avoid assumptions, maintain good and open communication, and show love indefinitely.

CHAPTER 5: MINDFUL HABITS

Make communication strong by sharing healthy habits with your couple. You can do that by coming up with a list of healthy habits in everyday life. Change your focus. A great way to do this is mindfulness, a non-judgmental presence at the moment. Mindfulness will control those wild running horses; studies show that meditation can reduce cognitive and emotional and bias.

Common practices of healthy couples
"What makes a relationship healthy?" It can be challenging to spot the signs when you're enjoying mind-blowing sex, handmade cards, and romantic dinners. I took a look back at the things I have done (and had done to me) to present you with the mindful practices of healthy couples.

- **You use sex to connect, not to fill a void**

As someone who has tried to find happiness externally in the past, I was never truly aware of why I craved for affection. I have since learned that it is crucial to understand why you need affection and when you need it. Do not be brainwashed and think that having good sex will make you feel validated or address underlying challenges. That needs to be worked out with a coach or therapist, not in our sleeping room.

- **You choose to see the best, not the worst**

We choose where we want to place our attention. And as the saying goes, where attention goes, energy flows. In every situation you have two options:

✓ You can nitpick and use that as an excuse to end the relationship, or
✓ You can choose to appreciate what's good about your significant other.

What are the things that make you love and appreciate your partner? Take a trip down memory lane and remember the funny jokes, hikes, and adventures. This isn't to say you should deny reality, but it's a tool to help you work on the relationship from a place of love rather than fear.

Ultimately, if you look for what he does wrong, you can always find something. If you look for what he does right, you can find something, too. It all depends on what you want to look for. Happy couples accentuate the positive.

- **You see things in the present rather than generalizing patterns**

In a healthy relationship, each person avoids making grandiose statements like "You always..." or "You never..." One instance of doing something that you don't like doesn't define your partner or his behavior throughout the relationship. It's easy for us to want to lump things into patterns, but when you've put an issue to rest, mass generalizations open up old wounds. Treat each instance as a unique event unless you're sure you want to end it.

- **You take responsibility for your growth rather than using the relationship as an excuse to avoid growth**

In a healthy relationship, you take space to pursue a life outside of your partner. After all, he signed on for a partner, not a groupie. In an unhealthy relationship, you define yourself through that union, losing touch with your authentic self. Relationships are spiritual assignments, helping us to evolve into who we're meant to be. When the relationship gets in the way of that, it's time to reevaluate your situation.

- **You communicate what you want instead of what you don't want**

There's a difference between a complaint and a constructive comment. In a healthy relationship, you communicate what you want. For example, it's much more humane to say "I want us to spend time with my family" rather than saying "We spend too much time with your family and not enough with mine." Your positive approach will help put your partner at ease rather than signaling that he should prepare for war.

- **You're open and honest instead of passive-aggressive**

Saying "whatever you want" may squash a problem now, but it creates a pattern of apathy and resentment. In a healthy relationship, you take responsibility for your decisions and healthily communicate them.

- **You show love every day, not only on special occasions**

I once dated a guy who felt that saying "I love you" often would cheapen its meaning. He preferred to save it for special occasions. A healthy relationship is based on a pattern of positive connection, creating intimacy and positive expression. Each party acknowledges and recognizes the other daily. It does not have to be elaborate, but it does have to be sincere, for example, "You are a wonderful friend." In a healthy relationship, love is expressed with gestures, acts, and words.

- **You spend time together**

Quality time together connects both people. It does not have to be formal. For many people, intimacy is developed through the conscious connection. For example, reading the newspaper at the same time, exercising together, or sharing your morning routine. It is about quality time, not the amount of time. Someone can be great on paper, but without those little moments each day, his or her resume does not hold water.

- **You don't take all his choices personally**

I once argued with my partner over his lifestyle choices, believing that he needed to address his love of cigarettes, pizza, and burgers for us to be a happy couple. As much as I liked to rationalize my arguments; the truth is that he is the one who had to deal with the effects, not me. Things are only your problem when you make them your problem. And while it is your choice to accept his life decisions and choose whether or not you can live with them, it is vital to remember not to take them on a personal level.

While there are many methods to detect an unhealthy relationship, it comes down to connecting with yourself. Are you your authentic self in this relationship? Are you making heart-centered decisions? A healthy love should leave you feeling comfortable, whereas unhealthy love leaves you feeling disconnected and drained.

CHAPTER 6: APPRECIATING AND ACCEPTING YOUR PARTNER

You should make it a habit to accept your partners for who they are. Learn how to appreciate and take your partner for what he or she is by not judging your partner. In a relationship between two people who are bound by love, in the beginning, one's partner is transformed into a picture of human perfection. As time goes by the perfection wears off, and each partner discovers how compatible they are, there is at least one thing that each partner dislikes of the other partner. Each partner has a behavior, habit or personal trait that annoys or disappoints the other partner.

As the love story of the two partners goes ahead, they fall in love very much with each other, but their quirks may become a reason for perpetual conflict at home. These failures may often make the other partner feel disappointed and even may end up causing contempt, for the other partner. This may lead to a partner wanting the other partner to change a specific behavior; this may cause a serious feud between the two partners that may end up causing a rift between them. That may also hinder their communication in the committed relationship. For this to work, it is simple, each partner needs to accept that their partner is never going to change and the only way to beat this is by accepting your partner for who they are in every aspect.

Tips on how to accept your partner for who they are in a committed relationship

- **Respecting your partners' beliefs and acknowledging their opinions.**

In a relationship, you don't need to have the same opinions or subscribe to similar beliefs with that of your partner all the time. You two are unique individuals, who are entitled to their definition of and reaction towards a situation in the environment around you. To accept your partner for who they are means acknowledging that you two will always disagree on several issues, but that doesn't mean that there is a need for an unhealthy reaction such as violence.

- **Accept your partners' imperfections while embracing their flaws.**

You need to accept your partner's significant emotional and physical weaknesses. For example, when your partner is more talented than you or they do not share your level of confidence when it comes to socializing. A partner needs to accept the other imperfection, and all these can be learned, is a matter of time. Accepting your partners' flaws does not mean that you let them hurt you because you still have hope in your partner that he/she will change someday. If a relationship reaches this point it can be toxic and hazardous that should not be tolerated at all.

- **Never force your partner to change to be better.**

It is very unfair for a partner to force the other partner to change the way of living their life. This is because we are unique individuals who are guided by different beliefs and also unique individuals who follow different paths in life. As a couple, you need to accept these differences, so long as their decisions and lifestyle will not hurt the other partner in the relationship. Respect and patience are all that is needed to deal with this, as they will grow up to becoming better persons with time.

- **Knowing your partners' story and what motivates them**

In some instances, one will never understand why they do what they do. With time some decisions will be confusing for one partner that may lead to the partner to question their sanity; this is because they do not agree with how the other partner wants things to be done. In this case, how do you deal with such a situation? One needs to know where his or her partner is coming from and the underlying reasons that made him or her what they are currently. You need to listen and know their story, and you also need to respect the lessons life has taught them. Trust is also essential in this situation, trust your partner for them to do the right thing not just because you love and care about them, trust them because you believe in their capabilities in life.

- **Do not compare your partner with other people from your past.**

You should never compare your current partner to your past love life or with the people you have met in the past. To some partner, this will only be a deal-breaker that may lead to them being hurt and worried. Love your partner for who they are now and please do not go looking for more. You should move on from your past and accept your partner in your present life. If this cannot be the case, then you do not deserve their everlasting love.

- **Love your partner for who they are from the inside**

You should ask yourself what made you fall in love with your partner in the first place? I hope it is what was inside them, their personality, their soul and heart, their smile and the little things that make them unique to you. As we all know that love is not blind it helps us to see what we have been missing in our love life: a special soul, a special heart, a unique soul and an unusual love that brings with it sincere and genuine joy and happiness in our days.

- **Being patient with your partner and giving them time to grow**

For a relationship to last, maturity makes a big difference in that relationship. In some relationship couples do not share the same level of experience and understanding; this may be caused by a gap in terms of their age difference. Despite your relationship being compatible as you may believe, sometimes a gap in age or difference in maturity can affect your relationship in a negative way. For you like the older person in the relationship and more experienced, you have the responsibility to wait for them to grow. You need to guide them through this passage and the learning process. Patience is necessary when guiding them to be the best person your partner was meant to be.

- **Being proud of your partner and show them you mean it**

Always be proud of your partner for what they have accomplished in their life and what they have become. Being aware of their past and struggles that they have faced, appreciate them and compliment them of what they have achieved, a job well done. The only acceptable way to show your partner that you accept them for who and what they are in a committed relationship is for you to be happy about the goals they have achieved and show to everyone that you are proud of your partners' achievements. Tell your partner that they are perfect in their imperfect ways that will be the sweetest and ideal act to show love to your partner.

Appreciating your partner in a relationship

After you have accepted your partner for who they are in a relationship, you should then appreciate your partner in a committed relationship. Being appreciative to your partner is one of the most beneficial activities you can do for your relationship. Appreciating your partner is fun and enriching. Verbal appreciation shows how much you adore your partner and shows you are committed to the relationship. It also shows that their efforts are appreciated no matter how small they may seem to be.

Showing value in a relationship is critical; this allows one to know where they stand in a relationship and also what they mean to you. When a partner in a relationship is dedicated, and yet they do not know how valuable they are to that relationship. This changes how that person operates and function in that union. When you do not show value to your partner, and they believe so, the other partner tends to devalue the relationship.

Here are the reasons why you should show your partner you appreciate them:

- It makes it easier for your partner to show you that they appreciate you also.

You need to show that you appreciate someone first before you are welcomed too. By doing so, it makes it easier for your partner to show appreciation to you also. The main reason as to why people tend to withhold recognition is that they do not feel recognized in the first place.

- Makes your partner feel happy

Most people tend to feel happy when they do things for other people. They derive happiness by them being generous in giving or offering services to other people. This may change when this type of people do not get any sign of appreciation of what they are doing. They become disgruntled about doing so. Some act, do not need any payment, but by just simply telling them that you appreciate their act of kindness and their efforts, this makes them feel happy.

- Being appreciated makes them feel loved

Most often, people feel that the person they love does not love them back the same way they love them. You love your partner because of what you feel about them, so when you appreciate them, you are telling them how much you love them back.

- It makes your partner feel special

This makes a person in a relationship feel honored, treasured and special. You are telling your partner how much you mean to them and how important they are in that relationship. By doing so, your relationship will be based on a special ground that will make it stronger than ever.

- It shows that you respect your partner

Respect plays a bigger role in the success of a relationship. With no respect, a relationship is doomed to fail.

- It is a sign that you are grateful for what they do for you

When a partner receives appreciation from you, it motivates them to keep doing it. By them being motivated it creates a kind of consistency in the action they do, and nothing provides consistency like recognition.

Signs showing that your partner is not feeling appreciated in a relationship
1. Your partner is quicker to argue
2. Your partner is often sad.
3. Having a feeling of growing distance between the two of you.
4. Your partner becomes more quiet than usual
5. Your partner becomes more emotional than before
6. When your partner stops doing things they are used to do.

Naturally, when you put hard work into something, it is always a great thing to get a pat on the back for the efforts you have put. When you are more appreciative to your partner in a relationship and also being grateful for the contribution, your partner brings in your life, the happier the two of you will be as couples. Always remember to make appreciating to your partner as the priority.

Ways of showing your partner that you appreciate them
1. Expressing love to your partner often. Good relationships are those that evolve when it comes to love, appreciating your partner love will never be enough. It is always a consistent thing that needs to be revisited each time you are with your partner.
2. Always spend time together with your partner. Laugh together, be playful together and always have fun while you appreciate each other.
3. Often compliment your partner even on little things. For example "that red dress makes you look vibrant. I love it; my dear."
4. Always acknowledge the things that make you love your partner. -for example their friend or their family.
5. Appreciate your partner for always being there for you, in your ups and challenging moments of your life. Your partner is the person who invests most of their time on you, more than any other person in your life.
6. By appreciating your partner, it shows them that you do not take them for granted in any way.
7. Always thank your partner for the small things that make a big difference in your life -for example ironing your clothes, preparing food for you and washing dishes for you.
8. Paying total attention to your spouse when they are talking to you about any matter that affects you two. Ensure that you make full eye contact when you are having a conversation with your partner, this shows that you are paying full attention and you are serious about the matter.

Importance of showing appreciation to your spouse
- A partner who shows appreciation in a relationship is more committed to the relationship and is more likely to stay in the relationship for long.
- A partner who savors his/her present or past has a greater joy in the relationship than those who do not savor their past or present situations.
- By eliminating positive events mentally, one can spur appreciation. This type of strategy helps one to improve their positive emotions and their well-being.
- When a partner attempts to foster appreciation by them comparing themselves with others, it boosts both negative and positive emotions. Always remember to be very cautious when you are drawing

- comparisons to others in a relationship.
- Being appreciative is not all positive. In some cases, appreciation can lead to lowering one's aspirations. This happens when you draw attention away from future possibilities. So it's always advised to be mindful of a balance between aspiration and appreciation in one's life.
- Gratitude towards your partner is associated with stronger ties in a relationship, greater willingness in the partner to share concerns in the relationship and it also creates a higher level of marital satisfaction.

Replacing judgment with compassion in a relationship
Every person always has a dream to be in a relationship that they feel entirely free from judgment and safe. Sometimes a couple finds themselves regularly clashing, judging one another for their poor actions or decisions. This constant argument between them only cause division or forms a larger wedge space between them, instead of creating intimacy and love between them. For you to stop judging your partner, take time and eliminate the judgmental thought that you have in your mind and instead replace it with a sense of gratitude that your partner is always there for you, for better or for worse.

Create a feeling of compassion for your partner instead of the judgmental thought. For example, when your spouse arrives late home from work, instead of negative, judgmental views about them, you need to frame your thoughts into compassion for him/her, for having a long day at work.

This kind of reaction is called Radical Acceptance. Radical Acceptance is powerful, beautiful and most importantly transformative practice. Most importantly you need to commit to the intention and to merely be aware of when you are judgmental to your partner, and the need to call yourself out appropriately.

Finally, it is vital to accept and appreciate your partner as they are and for what they bring in your life. Always focus on the positives in your relationship; this will create a stronger bond between couples. Challenges in the relationship always arise, but the best way for the two of you to deal with the problems is both you to have a candid and sincere conversation about the negatives in your relationship. This will allow both of you to come up with an agreement and how to deal with the situation amicably.

By couples accepting and appreciating each other, it will create a good environment for the couple to communicate more openly without holding anything back.

CHAPTER 7: THE EGO MONSTER

Ego is the most dangerous thing in relationships; eliminate your ego to get a neutral point of view.

The term ego refers to when a partner in a relationship feels the entitlement of things to be done their way. People develop ego because they think they are superior to others. In a love relationship, when you turn and let your ego to make crucial decisions in your relationship rather than your spirit, this will lead to manipulation as a means to give and receive love. This is because the ego does not have any relationship skill. Whenever you try to protect yourself, ego resorts to fighting, sarcasm, depression, aggression, intolerance, blame, resentment, distrust, frustration, rude gestures and self-doubt.

Choices that we make out of our ego end up being the very obstacle to our relationship and love life. This, in turn, ends up being ego battleships instead of the committed relationship between two persons.

For natural love in a relationship, there is no need for manipulation to receive or give love. One's spirit loves, and it is capable of loving with no conditions or expectations. Our spirits also utilize the relationship skills of wisdom, acceptance, forgiveness, apologizing, being creative, being responsible, understanding and being discerning.

Signs of egoism in a relationship

- **Losing yourself.** This happens when one gives up their desires, hobbies, values, and even, at times, family and friends to please another individual. By doing so, we allow the ego to get love. You might think that the only way to get love from another person is by you to alter yourself into something that the other person wants; this is ego operating. The more you pretend to be something that you are not, the less loved you will feel. Hence, approval becoming the only hurdle in you receiving the love.
- **Constant judgment and criticism.** When you act out of your ego, you may think that the best way to love someone is by changing them, the effort of love becomes the need for control.
- **A partner that needs to be always right.** When one allows their ego to be in control of their feelings and in the way of love, this individual will always choose themselves, and they will always feel the need to be right above anyone else even their spouse.
- **A partner that needs to be always in control.** This occurs when a

partner feels the need to have overwhelming control over the other partner in a relationship. You may end up putting your own needs above the needs of the other person. This allows one partner to choose what and how they believe things should be done over love.
- **Shutting down your partner in the middle of a conversation.** Allowing ego to take control makes one not to respect the opinions or views of the other person. Ego will make you feel the need to shut down the opinion of your partner especially if their opinion differs with your opinion. This is the worse level of intolerance in a committed relationship.
- **A partner will refuse to talk about some specific topics in life.** A partner with a strong ego will tend to avoid discussion of topics that they do not want. The need for a partner to decide what is acceptable and that which is not acceptable is an act of one partner; this should not be the case because of the concept of two as a couple, not one.
- **A partner will refuse or hold back to solve a misunderstanding.** People with strong ego will tend to stay angry in an argument for a long time, and this does not bother them at all. They do not feel the importance of solving the matter as soon as possible. Extreme ego tends to make a decision that is against the wishes of the person they love.

How ego can kill a relationship
One of the biggest challenges we have in our relationships is that most people get into a relationship to get something they desire. This kind of people tends to find someone who will make them feel good according to their desire. Naturally, a relationship is a place where you go to give, and not a place where you go to take.

You should accept and give importance to others rather than allowing ego to consume you and ignore the importance of the other partner in a relationship. Every human being is different and so do their opinions differ. It is difficult to accept the opinions of others or make a compromise on them. In a relationship, if you do not do so, this will kill a relationship. Having self-respect is ideal for all, when you give importance to your partner, appropriately attend to him/her and show them the affection that is needed. Attitude is a factor that can help in solving a problem in a damaging relationship.

The most important part of interaction is the ability to listen to other person views first before reacting. When a partner has filled themselves with ego, during an interaction it will be difficult for them to listen to the other partner; this is because ego has made them feel superior to their partner.

One's ego can ruin a conversation with your spouse
In most cases people allow their pride to take over a conversation. You may think that you are too smart to even listen to the other person. We may also think that we are better than the other person and we have nothing more to learn from them. When you close yourself from listening to other people, you are doomed; this is because you stop learning. For you to eliminate this listening barrier, you have to be more open-minded, by learning from other people and also by listening to other people views and opinions. It costs you nothing by just listening; you do not need to agree with everything that is said.

Signs showing that ego is destroying your relationship
- Others are better than you. Ask yourself are you playing the victim card in your relationship? Are you comparing yourself to your partner? Do you put yourself down to get a rise? You will realize that ego will always partake in negative reinforcement rather than in positives reinforcement. If you are doing the above habits, you need to step back and reexamine your relationship.
- Jealousy. This is a monster that provides the greatest platform of drama in a relationship. Ego thrives well in lack of self-acceptance and self-worth. When you allow jealousy to engulf your relationship you are allowing jealousy to create the highest form of toxic energy in your relationship. If you are in an abusive relationship, ego will make you maintain this type of relationship through jealousies. If your partner is making you question the relationship, then you need to raise the red flag to step back and be sincere with the kind of abusive relationship you are in.
- Having a fear of rejection. This kind of fear makes you not achieve any goal that you had set, and by doing so, you are doing injustice to your relationship. Ego creates this fear in a person, instead of listening to the voice of ego and fear, you need to shift your perception from the ego's anxiety and to nag to a constructive way to gain self-confidence that you will achieve whatever you had set no matter what. Remember that your ego thrives when you have negative self-talk. An intimate relationship is built upon mutual acceptance and admiration. When you feel rejection to your partner, then it's time for you to analyze your commitment with your partner.
- Feeling that you must have the last word. Turning everything in a relationship to be a one-man play, this is a cause of ego in a relationship. When you realize that you and your partner have excessive discussions without asking about the other, well that is a sign that you are in an ego-driven relationship. Ego plays a crucial role in ensuring that you do not achieve complete happiness and peace. Ego also creates a scenario that

does not naturally exist, for example when you find yourself to be always having the last say on everything, it is time for you to step back and find the root cause.
- Constant blaming. This happens when you find yourself always blaming your partner for everything. You need to know that in a relationship it is about a couple two people and not one person. This is caused by our ego in a relationship. Ego is controlling your relationship and use manipulation to make it work. Ego loves to criticize and blame. When one does not take responsibility for their actions in a relationship, ego will use this to project to another negative situation.

How to control your ego and improve your relationship
The following techniques can help you learn how to let go of your ego:

- **Practicing letting go and forgiveness.** One of the most powerful tools that will help you in letting go of your ego is to practice forgiveness. You need to learn how to forgive people who hurt you and also learn how to forgive yourself. By forgiving, you will be able to accept, let go and keep moving forward to achieve your set goal. Forgiveness will allow your soul to remove the negativity in our inner being and allow a new wave of happiness in our soul.
- **Practicing being open and honest.** One of the most important statements that I know we have all come across in our day to day routine is "The truth will set us free." Holding onto the truth will suppress your emotions that will make you develop depression and anxiety. Being honest will always provide you with unconditional freedom for you to be connected with yourself instead of you trying to be something that you are naturally not. Learn to say No to the things or matters that do not add value to your life, accept and open your arms to things that bring positive impact in your life.
- **Learn to Surrender Your Need to be always in Control.** When you let your ego control your love relationship, it will always make you conform to things or Statue that is not part of your natural being. By doing so, you do things that you are not used to doing, and when you lose one of the things that you have created to make yourself what you want, you will realize that all the other things that you identify yourself with will fall like dominos and this will lead to you losing your happiness. Do what makes you happy as a person, be curious and be a risk taker. Take a challenge every day and do something that scares you and notices that you will start to feel happy in the small things that you do.
- **Having silent moments to yourself and enjoy it.** Create a daily routine that reminds you of how special you are and why it is beautiful

for you to be yourself. In the same daily routine perform an act of self-love and enjoy doing it. Five minutes every day for you to be alone and in silence. Sometimes in silence, you may find answers that in noise or voices can never find.
- **By practicing gratitude.** Create time for yourself every day for you to think about all the experiences, lessons and mistakes that you have achieved in your day to day life and be thankful to all those. In life, it is about the challenges we face and how we react to them that makes us succeed and be happy in life. People who are always appreciative tend to feel more loved and compassion, compared to people who are consistently not grateful of any deed since they live in self-denial. This is a breeding ground for the ego to thrive and other negative thoughts. Showing appreciation will also show you the beauty of life.

The battle of love versus ego

As human beings, we all have an ego within us. All we need to do is to learn to control our ego and not to let it control our lives. Letting your ego go unchecked can cause tremendous turmoil in your life especially with our closest and intimate relationships. Having negative emotions, for example, fear, jealousy, and anger are all products of ego. We all have two opposing forces that battle against each other in our inner being. In a battle, each side always has its agenda, idea, and suggestions. The forces are always opposite one another. These two forces in us are the force of Ego and the force of Love. It is upon you to choose which one will control or govern your life.

How the battle unfolds

1. **The force of ego.** This kind of force makes you decide with the help of your ego rather than your spirits. The negative thing about the force of ego is that it has no any relationship skill. Instead, it uses manipulation to receive love and give love. The force of ego makes one have fear, that loving will result from hurting, and it also creates a fear that if you love so much, you will abandon the concept of ego, that is self-protection and separation. Ego Love is a mirror of the desire and need of the lover and not the loved one. This kind of love only rests on the mercy of one partner, the partner that is being manipulative to receive the love. It asks them to be something that they cannot possibly be, that is what you want them to be, rather than what they are. This practice leads to disappointment and disillusionment that will lead to resentment. All in all the Genesis of all these things will lead to breaking up of a relationship.
2. **Force of love.** This is a force that drives us towards good deeds. It ensures one to be always sensitive and kind at all times. It admonishes you when you are neglectful and unkind to your partner or people close to you. In this kind of love, there are no demands that are placed to the

other partner compared to the Ego Love. This is because in this Love force there are no demands. With no demands on this kind of love, there are no expectations from any party. This kind of love takes ego out of our hearts; it controls every aspect of our life and every move that we make, hence creating beauty and joy wherever we go.

How you can deal with a person with a huge ego
1. Do not be afraid to be a little rude to someone you know has a big ego.
2. Try not to make any sense out of their behavior; this is because someone with a huge ego tends not to make any sense.
3. When they do not even agree with you on normal facts, please just don't try to argue with them.
4. When you are in a conversation with someone with a huge ego, talk facts and not emotions.
5. There is a need to cut some phrases from your speech, for example, do not try sentences with: I feel..., I think..., I just.... and I sort of...... This is because such phrases will automatically make you sound less superior to them.
6. At the start of any conversation with someone with a huge ego, it is advisable for you to adjust your attitude so as you are not expecting a crappy talk.
7. Always do not take it personally if they tend to use vulgar language or abuse you.

CHAPTER 8: LOVE UNCONDITIONALLY

The secret to having everything is not expecting anything. The concept of unconditional love in an intimate relationship is a noble course. We all want to be loved as we are and for what we are. You should love a person for who they are their personality traits and their ideologies. Without any conditions made, one would be able to bestow unconditional love to their partners.

Unconditional love comes with caring about the happiness of another person with no concerns of how it will benefit you as a person. This kind of love is similar to those who are involved in a maternal love or romantic love; this is connected or linked to the brains reward system. It shows that unconditional love is rewarding without receiving something in return.

Romantic unconditional love
This kind of love is based on whether adults who are involved in that relationship can also show each other this type of unconditional love. In this relationship you need to feel safe; it is sensible that you need to feel as though the other person will not leave you based on a whim. One needs to be assured that the other person is committed to loving them unconditionally despite what the future will bring. In romantic unconditional love, for love to continue existing, there should be mutual respect between the couple, not an attitude of your partner. In this case, you will put up with your partners' behavior and stick to them no matter what they do.

Positive unconditional love
In this kind of love, unconditional love does not mean that you always give people what they want or always accepting what they do, at the mercy of your personal needs. This is a kind of mature love that you treat the person that you love with respect while even maintaining your boundaries and protecting oneself. You recognize your main purpose; in the face of your partners' behavior, you pass your message with respect and love. This comes with being attuned and attentive, even while you set your boundaries you still mind the request of your partner and honoring them without hurting yourself.

This requires you not being dismissive and harsh as this will lead to no compromises. Communicating to your partner where you stand and your view on a certain issue, so that both of you can work out the best solution.

How to love unconditionally
This means that the couple should set their eyes on what keeps them together.

- **Embracing every moment you spend together.** Life is filled with ups and downs in a relationship. You are required to accommodate every

aspect of your partners' life including the ups and downs. No love is perfect; the sad part of it is as important as the good part of it.
- **Do not surrender at the site of imperfection.** Naturally, no one is perfect, that also applies to your partner he/she make mistakes. You both have obsessions, particularities, flaws, and different views. Even if your partner is not perfect, it doesn't mean he/she is not the right person for you. People with most easy-going attitudes also have quirks. You need to understand and learn that not you or your partner is perfect, but you both need to work things out to make it work for both of you.
- **Always strive to work through hard times.** Endurance, during your hard times, is very crucial to unconditional love. Do not allow the unfavorable and dark conditions fool you that you cannot be in the relationship that may lead you to give up. Always have the strength and right mentality to believe that your love is worth fighting for and work through the obstacles together. In the end, you come out victorious, and your relationship will come out stronger than ever.
- **Having mutual respect and striking a balance.** One should always work out a formula to divvy up responsibilities, chores, and tasks in a relationship. By doing so, you will have figured out a balance in your relationship. Relationships will always involve the aspect of giving and taking, hence no need to create a feeling of resentment in either one of the couple. You should make compromises for your partner and also allow your partner to make compromises for you; this will create Respect between the two of you.
- **Create a feeling of happiness that you and your partner deserve.** This is the most crucial aspect of unconditional love that is both of you deserve to be happy. No one would ever suggest being in a relationship that they feel they are unhappy. Having a belief that you and your partner deserve to be happy, will put you in the right direction. Some trials and tribulations come with putting together two different lives into one, these trials and tribulations need not be ignored but to be accepted wholeheartedly. Unconditional love will make your stay in that relationship and make it work to the best of your abilities.

How to know that you have found unconditional love
- Being able to freely express each other concerns, even when it feels to be uncomfortable.
- When you admit your failings, your partner will not judge you or shame you. Instead, they will hold your hand through recovery.
- When one gets vulnerable, the partner will respond with empathy and encourage the partner while trying to allay any fears.
- Forgiving each other freely with no conditions. Forgiving and completely

- forgetting.
- When you wrong your partner, you will actively pursue restitution and act on rebuilding your lost trust to your partner.
- No holding of grudges or pick up arguments over petty issues that can be talked through and be solved amicably. If it reaches a point of arguments, you respect each other and objectively resolve in a healthy resolution.
- When you do not need to prove anything or yourself to your partner
- When your partner sincerely places your needs before their own needs, without any expectations of receiving anything in return.
- Your partner takes time to encourage you and inspires you, for them to bring the best out of you or the best version of you.
- Celebrating each other successes while you appreciate them.
- Having a deep empathy towards your partner.
- Feeling safe when you are around your partner.
- When you both consider communication to be very important.

Unconditional love does not mean you are there no matter what you do
Many people may think from the definition of unconditional love that a person will stay in a relationship with a person no matter what they do. You might think that true love means overlooking all that your partner does and never giving up on them. This kind of myth can be hazardous and misguiding. It has caused very many people to stay in an abusive relationship, without them speaking up on what is happening to them in reality. They pretend everything to be working okay and in the right direction. Whatever your partner does every day affect your life positively or negatively, your emotions and also your feelings and your well-being hence the need of not overlooking your partners' actions in the name of unconditional love.

Unconditional love is not being codependent
Unconditional love means you support your partner no matter what happens to them; this is the contrast of them taking advantage of your love. They should not rely on you to meet all their emotional satisfaction. Nevertheless, everyone is responsible for their happiness. A relationship that is unhealthy, emotional reliance is codependency; this is not unconditional love.

A relationship is codependent when one partner: Relies too much on the other person to feel happy, you lose your identity, or when you no longer think that you are an independent party in the relationship.

Unconditional love is not all about your partner
As a human being, you have your flaws. You are not required to love every single flaw in your partner. Unconditional love means that you dislike a few

traits in your partner which is ultimately the nature of human beings. Being in love with every single character of your partner can imply that you are only focusing on the good qualities. You deny yourself the opportunity to believe that your partner could have anything negative about them.

Unconditional love does not mean over-protecting your partner
Fact is that no one would ever wish to see something terrible happening to the people they love. Having a desire to protect your partner is a natural response to the personal relationship we have with our loved ones. Though at times being overprotective might stand in the way of progress. A person would wish to see their partner take steps to improve their livelihood and for them to achieve the goals they have set in life. In the process of them making the steps, the process will be filled with risks and failures. It is with these failures and risks that disappointment and pain will manifest in that journey. By one loving their partner, you should understand that some of this pain can't be avoided and it is even necessary for the pain for them to get to where they want to be in life. So by being overprotective to them, you will hurt them in the process of protecting them so much or even hinder them from achieving the goals they had set.

True unconditional love allows a couple to change and grow as individuals overtime
In a relationship, love is viewed as shared personal values and desires in life. A couple should understand this will change over time. As the couple develops and works together to ensure they are a better couple and also better individuals in the future. The truth is that you are together because you want to support each other by making critical changes. You will want to see your partner grow and improve in their desires. When you notice an emotional distance growing between the two of you, this is because your values and traits do not align with the other person.

Developing at a personal level will help you begin to notice the difference, and this will help each partner to align their desire with the other partner. Unconditional love allows you to be joyful even when your partner is not around; this is because you have grown in person to improve your self-confidence. It makes you understand that you can be independent, even when each one of you is pursuing their desires.

It gives one certain freedom in a relationship. In this freedom, you need to be your person, have some personal time alone, have time to achieve your personal goals and live happily. When you can meet your set goals, you will have a better understanding of yourself. Understanding yourself, knowing yourself and loving yourself allow one to love another person or your partner unconditionally.

Unconditional love is not one-way
When your partner does not love you the same way you love them, it is not unconditional love this is what we call damaging self-sacrifice. You need to hold yourself to the same level that you expect your partner to hold you in and that you should make sure that they adhere to it. This is referred to as mutually supportive, meaning each partner pulls the other up to the healthiest way of loving and not either of the partners tearing one another down. You should consider asking your partner to love you more healthily and respectfully. Love acts reciprocally. This may sound like setting demands, but it understands your self-worth. This is the only way one can improve his/her relationship.

Relationship break down
Human beings are programmed to love conditionally. You love your partner due to his/her unique character traits and qualities. These are the traits that attracted you to them. These are the reasons why you love him/her and not any other person. The tricky part arises when the person you love changes in terms of the personal traits, if they change, at what level is love withdrawn?

True mature love comes with no strings attached. This kind of love is a behavior rather than a feeling. It reaches a point of confusion that leads to breaking down of the intimate relationship. Unconditional love satisfaction should arise from the act of giving it to the other partner, and not from what one will receive in return. When you think of unconditional love as an expression of our kindest being, then it can be maintained even when a relationship does not survive.

An example is when a couple still loves another despite them not being together. When you feel that a relationship is hurting you more, then that relationship is not good for you. It is perfect and advisable for you to feel the unconditional love but say goodbye to the relationship. This kind of love is basic in the goodness and total acceptance of someone; this does not mean that you should tolerate abuse, neglect or other deal breakers. When you first fell in love with your partner, the state at that point can be referred to as unconditional. But do not forget that we live in a conditional world where relationships do come to an end. This is because we all have different needs and choices that we make individually, and these desires and needs do change with time. Ties that completely lack unconditional love are unlikely to survive. Lifestyle and needs do change with time, if you are not ready and willing to see your partner go through a process of change, this could be a reason for the breaking of the relationship for the both of you.

A partner can be more important to the other person when they offer unconditional love in a mature sense. This is possible by one of the partners being mindful of the present situation. When you struggle by doing so, you should practice mindful meditation. Practicing mindful meditation will help you to slow down and be aware of your relationship needs. By doing so, it might also help you to learn how to show yourself the same unconditional love that you are trying to offer to you love partner. When one does not show themselves, unconditional love, first, it will be difficult for them to offer it to their partner.

Conditional love vs. unconditional love
Have you ever asked yourself if there is a difference between conditional love and unconditional love? The answer is yes.

In conditional love, you love someone conditionally; you tend to want your partner to act, look, and think in ways that fit your expectations and paradigms. This kind of love comes from your ego. You tend to hold your partner accountable for your expectations for them to qualify for your affection. In this kind of love, when your partner acts the way you want them to, you express your approval and satisfaction; if they act opposite to what you want them to do, you tend to withhold your expression of acceptance on them, and this is usually expressed in the form of anger. Conditional love polarizes your inner thoughts for you to believe that you are always right and your partner is ever wrong and that your partner should see things your way, not their way. You will always think entirely on the power play and try as much as possible to be in control of everything. This will trigger a defensive reaction from your partner.

When you look at conditional love in the aspect of sexual feelings, you will tend to find someone who will complete you or satisfy you rather than someone who you will share your whole-self with completely. When you act in a way that vastly deviates from your norm or natural expectations or you do something that hurts the people you love or your partner, this emotion can be completely transformed with time to move to the opposite spectrum which is hatred. If you find yourself at this point of hatred, you should step back and re-examine your relationship. Hatred is deeply rooted in fear and can cause real havoc in a relationship; it can be destructive on your emotional, mental, and physical well-being.

Comparing the conditional love to that of unconditional love, you will realize in unconditional love nothing is expected from your partner or the people you love. You will tend to reason with your spirit not as compared to conditional love where you will find yourself reasoning and making a decision based on your ego.

Unconditional love comes to you through the soul level. It starts at the level of self-forgiveness and self-acceptance. It will radiate divine light to your partner and everyone you love. Unconditional love will always have a positive impact on your emotional, physical, mental and spiritual well-being. When you open your heart to receive unconditional love, you will feel radiant and expansive; you will find yourself rising above the limitations of fear, this is because this kind of love is the most powerful force in existence.

CHAPTER 9: SET GOALS FOR YOUR RELATIONSHIP

In this chapter, you are going to learn about creating and setting real relationship goals. By doing so, you will be able to enhance and protect your love and also enhance communication with your partner or your spouse. You should have a reality check, ask yourself how much time do you spend nurturing and improving your love relationship? When you enter into a romantic relationship, you feel that the intoxicating fuel of infatuation will forever power your relationship at the same level. With time, the fuel runs low, and the relationship begins to hobble along on vapors. Some signs of such a point in the relationship are when the couple no longer has long chats getting to know how each other spent their day at work. The couple does not even get free time for them to spend together as it was the norm at the beginning of the relationship.

When it reaches this point, most couples do not know what to do, so they prefer not doing much or anything to revive their connection. How do you enjoy the profound satisfaction that is there in the long term committed relationship?

This can be achieved by understanding the stage of your relationship and setting mutual couple goals. This process will be a success by the commitment to daily actions to meet the best relationship targets for you and your partner or spouse.

What are these couple relationship goals?
Each person has a personal goal for their career, for their development, and self-improvement. As you have individual targets for personal growth, you and your partner can mindfully consider what is best for your relationship, creating and setting relationship goals, how the goals will be, and how both of you are going to achieve them. A committed relationship is an evolving connection which is also very dynamic due to the changes that occur over time. If both partners do not proactively think of what the future in that relationship should look like and how they can grow and evolve together despite the changes. Things might grow apart if the couple does not take drastic action.

These changes in life at a personal level may cause disconnection, unhappiness, and conflict. But all these can be avoided if the couple works together towards a common goal, remaining flexible as life changes arise, by doing so you might be able to protect your bond and enjoy all the benefits of relationship goals.

Relationship goals for couples to nurture and protect their bond
- **Prioritizing your relationship.** By being honest, most people tend to talk big about the importance of their marriage, but when it comes to reality when the rubber meets the road, they are not putting their relationship as the priority. As time passes by you, start taking one another for granted. One gets busy, and they get distracted with their stuff, and they neglect to check the desires of their partners. One should view the relationship as a given, a byproduct of his/her connection to the other person. You should know that a relationship is an entity of its own made up of three blocks that are, there is your partner, there is the relationship, and there is you. Comparing the three, the relationship is the first place that should be prioritized over everything else in your life. So setting the relationship as a goal should be a mutual goal, that both partners embrace it with open arms, as it is the centerpiece or the core of your life. How can you achieve this? Simple by just being committed to it every single day of your life, in all the decision that you make and actions that you take.
- **Creating a couple bubble.** This bubble reinforces the goal of prioritizing relationship by you thinking of "we" rather than "me." This goal tends to be very difficult for most couples; this is caused by the aspect of one viewing themselves as a team first above their independent habits and desires. Apart from the belief of being interdependence, that one's feel it is weakening them, in the real sense, it is strengthening you because each person feels cherished and a feeling of being safe is created. For you to achieve this particular goal, you need to make a series of mutual agreements with your partner that reinforces your care and protection of the relationship. This goal also involves you becoming an expert on your partners' needs, fears, and desires, quickly repairing damage to the relationship. By having a reservoir for happy events in your life, these memories counter any difficulties and also act like a rock in times of difficulty.
- **Having daily time for connection.** This is a fundamental daily goal for a couple. You should set time daily for one-on-one time together to reconnect. The most important aspect of this goal is that you can be there in person for your partner. You are focused on each other with no distractions. For couples who work outside the home, this is a very important goal for the couple to set. Make it a habit to do this early in the morning before the workday start or in the evenings before both of you are pulled away to responsibility and chores. You should not take this time to work through conflicts. No, you should take this time to talk, share, embrace and simply enjoy each other's company. The connection time should not be long hours; this should take to about twenty minutes

to twenty-five minutes.
- **Communicating to your partner with kindness.** In setting a common couple goal, you must include the ways you communicate with your partner. Avoid using covert words and behaviors that are profoundly wounding; this over time will accumulate enough to cause serious problems in your relationship. One loses trust, mutual respect and finally, the love is lost. One should make it a purpose in their goal to be kind during communication with your partner. Being kind during communication doesn't mean that you are obliged to agree with each other's sentiment.
- **Embracing Vulnerability.** We all have vulnerabilities that we tend to hide from our partners so as they don't think less of us. In a relationship, as intimacy and trust grow, this is the time you should share some of your vulnerabilities with your partner. This will help you find a place of security and safety, where you can offload your baggage in life, and you can, at last, be yourself completely. Having a sense of security and safety with your vulnerabilities is with your partner. By doing this, you can strengthen the bond between you and your spouse. This also fosters a deeper state of intimacy and love. When you treat the vulnerabilities of your partner with dignity, this can heal wounds from a past event and make you feel more confident of who you are. Make it a purpose for you to be completely open, real to each other and vulnerable.
- **Maintaining a satisfying sex life.** Despite you having a greater sex life with your partner at the beginning of your relationship, with time, this will grow to a boring or even burdensome from time to time. This can be avoided by you understanding your partners' needs that are related to sex as well as acknowledging your desires. Men are more visually stimulated and variety as compared to women. For women, they need to feel secure and comfortable with their sex partner for them to be willing to try new things and for them to be sexually adventurous.
- **Always plan to have fun together as a couple.** For a couple, the relationship should be a place of peace and a place to rest from the daily tribulations or your day to day routine. It should provide you with an outlet for enjoying and having fun to the fullest with your partner. Your life has been stressful and serious, with your days spent at work, taking care of your children, carrying out one to another errand and also dealing with daily situations. Your relationship is the place where you can run and have a humble resting opportunity. Try and bring back the early memories you had with your partner when you first met, the amount of time you spent together and the fun you had together. Couples should practice playing a couple of games and having fun together; this increases bonding and communication between the couple and

relationship satisfaction. Purpose to create time every week for you and your partner to have fun and enjoy together.
- **Supporting each other's personal goals.** As important as having a couple of bubble relationship goal, it is also important for you and your partner to have personal goals and dreams of your own. By having personal goals as a couple, you should not undermine your connection as a couple. This should strengthen your relationship as each one of you has a unique and promising idea to bring to the relationship. You should both know that the most important person in your life is your spouse or your partner, someone that admires and supports your goals and will always to see you succeed in all your set targets.
- **Having a yearly review.** When you and your spouse have time to set and create common goals, you should also create time to measure the level of success of your efforts. Sit down at the end of the year; discuss each of the goals you had set for your relationship. Ask yourselves the following questions
    - How successful have you been in achieving your goals?
    - What are the steps you have taken in the past to actualize your goals?
    - What are the areas that you need to work on to actualize your common couple desires?

Ensure that you have used this time well to come up with new goals for the coming year, which build on what you had already achieved in the previous year.

Long-term relationship goals

There will always be evolution and changes in your relationship as time goes by and all that you want as a couple is for your love and closeness to withstand the test of time. When you and your partner have real relationship goals that you have set, this will act as a buffer to caution you against the challenges that often come with the changes over time. The cushion or buffer also protects the relationship from being torn down apart. Having set a couple of goals, it encourages you and your partner to set the bar high for your relationship rather than allowing your connection to erode and wither with time.

Here are some ways in which you and your partner will achieve the above common couple goals:

- Ensure that the goals you have both sets make you feel good about yourselves. You can't achieve something opposite of your values. Sharing your couple's goals can be beneficial to others as well as yourselves, as it will act as a powerful bonding experience.

- Having talks as a couple of where you need to be in the next six months to one year. Keep it positive.
- You need to make sure that your personal goals are in line with your couple relationship goals. The alignment is essential since it will help both of you to achieve your dreams. This also creates harmony between your couple relationship goals and your personal goals.
- You should ensure that your goals are attainable and specific.
- Always make sure that you have celebrated any achievements or milestone reached as a couple. This is a simple way to motivate both of you.
- You should stay accountable to all the commitments you made to each other. This should be so since this is a sacred bond between the partners and it is not a matter of punishment or reward. This is an arrangement that supports both of you as well as your relationship.

Reasons for setting common couple goals
1. They act as the glue that holds you together, even during the most challenging moments in your relationship.
2. It provides great satisfaction when goals are achieved, and it gives spouses reasons for them to celebrate together.
3. Goals validate desires and hold one accountable to each other.
4. Setting common goals improves communication since each person in the relationship is given a chance to talk about personal goals and dreams; by doing, so it helps the couple to understand each other better.
5. Helps the spouse or partner to strengthen their relationship by working together to achieve the common goals.

A few years ago, at the suggestion of a friend, Troy and I began the tradition of setting goals for our marriage at the beginning of each New Year. We have always set goals for our family, finances, fitness, business, and parenting, but as we began to grow as a couple, we recognized several areas for improvement and began to set ourselves marital goals.

It is common to set goals at work to increase productivity and, on a personal level, to improve health or achieve something of importance like financial security. We know the value of working towards goals because we've witnessed what can be accomplished when we're focused and driven. So why not set goals for our marriage, as well?

Setting goals together as a couple requires you to work as a team towards a common purpose which helps fortify your relationship. From day one, Troy has referred to us as a team. I love this concept because it is so easy to relate to and understand.

If a team wants to win, each player has to work together with the others, to do it. In marriage, your ultimate goal is to help one other become holy and get to heaven, but I think most couples would agree that being in a fulfilling, happy marriage is a WIN on this side of heaven!

So how do we WIN in marriage? Life happens; we get knocked down and sometimes forget that we are on the same team! Don't overlook the fact that you are on the same team if you want to win. Remembering this motivates me to get beyond a grudge I may be holding and move more swiftly towards reconciliation. Determine what you can do daily or even weekly to reinforce the fact that you are on the same team. Perhaps, similar to doing a daily examination of conscience, you can do a marital examination of conscience, either privately in your heart or together as a couple. Reflect on what you did well that day/week to love your spouse and what areas need improvement.

Come up with a marital game plan. Every team has a plan they try to follow that puts them in the best position to win. Good offense – what can you proactively do to help your marriage grow? Good defense – what hedges do you need to put around your marriage to protect it from damage?

Teammates are accountable to one another. If one teammate is in the wrong, it affects the entire team. It is the same in marriage: it is important to forgive but also to hold each other accountable. There is a difference between holding a grudge and holding your spouse accountable for a wrong that needs to be made right. Until this is done, your team cannot work in sync. If you desire a successful marital team, you need to admit when you are wrong. Your spouse shouldn't have to pull an apology out of you; it takes away the sincerity of it. Admit when you are wrong, so you don't have to play defense without purpose. If you are the spouse that is offended, forgive to get out of the offensive zone. Make it a goal to be accountable to one another for the sake of your marriage, your family, and your salvation.

In any team, when one player is down, another player steps up to the plate to fill in. A good goal you may choose to set for your marriage is to understand better how you can support your spouse when he or she is down. Are you loving and emotionally supportive? Do you help pick them up or do you ignore the fact that they are down, so you don't have to deal with it? Perhaps, because of your wounds, pride or lack of energy, you find it challenging to help your spouse when he or she is down in their game. This is when relying on the grace of the sacrament of marriage gives you the strength to live your vows "in good times and in bad."

I recently read a story about an experiment off the coast of Brazil. Two bottles were dropped in the ocean off a boat at the same time and right next to each other. One bottle washed up on the coast of Ecuador 100 days later and the other bottle went across the Atlantic Ocean and washed up on the coast of Tanzania a year later. The bottles started in the same place but ended up a half a world apart. It is the same in marriage – it is so easy to drift apart and not even realize you are doing it! Setting goals together and following through on their development will help you consciously stay close so that you do not end up half a world apart. If you want to prevent drift in your relationship, you must be intentional.

Can you set a goal to have a weekly date night or get away together for a few days? Troy and I try to go on a date at least 2-3 times a month, and we also get away somewhere alone once a year for a few days. This "date" time has been an enormous blessing for our marriage!

Set realistic goals and be flexible. Do what works for you and be mindful of the current season. Periodically take time to reevaluate your goals and redesign your plan if necessary. Life happens, and inevitably, something will cause you to get off track, but the critical thing to remember is to get back on track as soon as possible and make accommodations if a curveball is thrown your way. Celebrate your accomplishments.

Goal setting as a couple improves communication and assists couples in better understanding one other because it allows each spouse to express their dreams and desires for the marriage. There is less misunderstanding, resentment, and conflict since each person is heard and their needs validated. This, in turn, leads to a more fulfilling and happy marriage.

CHAPTER 10: GROW TOGETHER

You should make it your priority to evolve together, expecting each other in difficult times continually. Good communication is the key when it comes to growing together. Good communication involves spouses showing each other that they are listening. Having a conversation with someone who is utterly quiet can make one feel that they are conversing with themselves.

It is, therefore, important that every spouse contributes to show they are listening. For example, a spouse may add on to what the other person has said. This shows that everyone is listening attentively and processing the issues. If, for example, one person is talking about their day at work, the partner may say, "It sounds as if that office has some people with personal issuers rubbing off on everybody. The things that the secretary said would tick me off too". The person may also add "What can I do to make your day better." Language like this shows a partner that they have been understood and that they can get help if they need it.

Good communication is not all about talking and talking. Sometimes, the best medicine involves a good level of silence. For instance, when two people are having a conversation, they can take a break to digest what they have said to each other. The silence will help the two people put their thoughts in order and avoid blunting out things unintentionally. Open communication and conversation do not mean going on and on in an endless conversation. Take a break and a breath. Good silence also indicates to the partners that they are reflecting on all that has been said.

Good and open communication requires one to be sensitive to the moods, schedules, and other factors of their partner. Select a good time to have an effective back and forth based on the conversation you want to have. However, things that need to be addressed should not be ousted too far off. Address matters openly as soon as possible because dwelling on them in silence will bring problems. One should pick a suitable moment as soon as possible and open up.

Another important factor that can help couples grow together is honoring the opinions of a partner even if they differ. Honoring different views is one of the main keys to good communication. To show honor of different opinions, one may say "I understand what you are saying, but I think... Can we agree to disagree?" Such statements will not only acknowledge that one person has understood the other but also that they respect a different opinion. They also help one state their different opinion without overstepping their boundaries.

Honoring the views of each other de-escalates what could have become a conflict.

Couples need to identify ways of having the most productive conversations which will add value to their marriage. One of the best ways of maintaining an emotional connection is through holding good open conversations. Couples should segregate time to hold conversations and put some of the tips named above into practice. Six secrets that couples can use to grow together include:

- ✓ **They evaluate experiences**

"Experience is the greatest teacher" only if we assess them and consciously learn from our mistakes. Otherwise, we are likely to repeat them. In growth-oriented marriages, couples take that crucial step back and ask: What worked in this situation? What didn't work? What can we do better next time? They stop arguing. They stop paddling. They come up with a new plan.

- ✓ **They learn to communicate in each other's language**

We all grow up with different communication styles and inferences. Some of us are used to families where everyone directly expresses his feelings, and others are used to more round-about, sensitive ways of speaking. The key to growing in marriage is to learn to speak your spouse's language even if that isn't how you are used to communicating. We often have to learn and re-learn this habit, sometimes to listen when our instinct is to speak, to pause before we figure out how to say something and to think about what we're trying to accomplish with our words.

- ✓ **They share what they learn**

Whether it is an exciting story in the news, an idea from a Torah class they heard or something new that they learned at work, couples who grow together share what they learn each day. They make sure to discuss ideas and goals so that their connection doesn't become lost in errands, to do lists and family responsibilities.

- ✓ **They see their relationship as multi-dimensional**

There are many ways I identify who I am. Part of my identity is associated with my profession as a family therapist and as a writer. A substantial portion of who I am is an amalgam of being an athlete, a mother, a wife, and a religious Jew. All of these parts of me are essential to my identity and reinforce each other. A growing marriage has several dimensions to its identity too. There is the romantic dimension that first drew the couple together, the friendship that becomes stronger each year, the team identity we need for parenting, and the shared activities dimension in which growing couples hike or bike or attend a class together. Like the parts of our personalities, the aspects of a growing marriage strengthen and enhance each other.

✓ They know how to laugh together
Life can sometimes get very stressful. Your kids are fighting. Your teenager doesn't like school. An appliance breaks. There's an extra hour of traffic... the list can go on and on. We all have stress and challenges. One of the best tools growing couples use for stress is humor. They know how to laugh to break the tension. They know how to step back and see the big picture when things get hard. They have jokes that they share so that they can find the way forward, even when they're stuck in traffic.

✓ They plan adventures together
Growth-oriented couples love to try new things and go to different places. It doesn't take a lot of money to go camping together or to hike in a state park or watching the sunset over the ocean. But it takes enthusiasm and a desire to grow for couples to reach new realms in their lives and their marriages.

The importance of practicing day after day to achieve a mindful relationship

Communication in marriage and connection are directly related. Without one, the other is likely to fail. When people can express themselves adequately, things tend to be better even when they cannot agree on a particular subject. For instance, if a couple is talking about how much money they should spend on entertainment per month, the husband may want more to go to movies and games while the wife wants more to go with her girlfriends for shopping sprees. The couple may not initially agree on the amount they should spend, but so long as they are communicating about it, they both understand what the other wants. When communication is a challenge, one may feel that the other is being wasteful and still not express it in the right way. Bad communication leads to feelings of isolation, sadness, loneliness, heartbroken and disheartened.

Communication is important for both simple and tough reasons. In the movies, couples seem to have some almost perfect lives, but in the real world, it is more complicated than that. People have to make decisions about children, money, work life, obligations, and other action items without a screen script to follow. Such matters call on the couples to have deep conversations. Even the little things that could be ignored before the couple lives together have to be taken into consideration; otherwise, the marriage might fail. Without the right communication in marriage, drifts happen, and the couple that was ones so in love becomes strangers sharing a table. Again, communication in marriage differs from communication in a relationship because couples tend to get tired of the masks want to deal with real feelings. The spouses want to be heard; their deep needs start to surface; they want to be validated. If one person keeps dismissing, interrupting or shutting down their partner, there will be a rift between them.

Good communication leads to a great marriage and more. As seen earlier, communication and connection go together and consequently if one goes down, the other fails too. Every couple should strive to revive the communication whenever there are hiccups because it will lead to stronger intimacy both physically and emotionally. Communication is not required in marriage just for emotional and physical connection. The couples also need to make decisions about development and growth.

In many cases, development and growth involve making decisions about money. When two people come together in marriage, there are a lot of emotions that get tied up in how they spend money. If therefore the couple keeps pushing aside conversations about money decisions, a lot of problems will arise soon in the family. Communication is also important because people only have a finite amount of time on earth- no one wants to be in a relationship where there is no connection. That is why many people opt for divorces when the spouses are no longer connected. One way to avoid separations and stay connected for a long time is to keep rediscovering things about one another more so through communication. Change for the better and show it to one another that you are putting effort to make it work. Share experiences, create new memories which you can discuss later and laugh. Good communication ensures that the couple knows which statements would make the other person shut down or build a wall; therefore, they avoid offending one another. Good communication is proactive such that, instead of waiting for things to go wrong to start a conversation, the couple sorts things out in time. The results of good communication are a solid foundation in the marriage where the couple can talk about anything without fear.

Many couples who have difficulties in communication think that it will take an arm and a leg to get back on track. Although this might be true for some broken communications, the majority of the couples need to make small steps towards better communication, and they will achieve a considerable difference. A few adjustments to the channels of communication and the spouses will achieve a tremendous compounding effect on their relationship and marriage. While facing communication challenges, many couples also tend to feel like they are the only ones undergoing this. It is important for them to remember that they are not the only ones facing challenges. Challenges are normal in every relationship. The key to solving the problems is consistency.

Remember, a distance between couples or any two people does not happen overnight. There is not just one reason which leads to a total drift in a couple that was once madly in love. It is a result of small omissions and commissions that offend the other person, therefore, creating mountains of differences and gaps between the two people. In the initial stages of a relationship and marriage, a couple can easily thrive on excitement and physical attraction, therefore, communication plays a small role and many of its aspects will be ignored.

As the bond between the two individuals deepens, the attraction changes very fast into the first stages of love where every person is making a foundation of trust. This is because they want to have a stronger and happier future. When in marriage, the love that once thrived on attraction and excitement changes to one that is sustained by trust, commitment, and honesty. Over the years, the responsibilities change, and the amount of stress increases with an increase in challenges. Somehow, the time to be there for one another and to share seems to diminish.

Communication becomes a chore that couples would rather skip even if it is talking about a joyous moment. Things seem to change, and the couples that thought marriage is a completely smooth ride usually feel cheated or lost. The suppressed negative feelings that arise from this situation make a couple preys to miscommunication or total lack of it. Then the drift occurs, followed by assumption and mistrusts, in worse cases infidelity, lack of respect, dishonesty, et cetera. Good communication means that a couple respects one another enough to stay honest.

Demystifying the fairytales

In all healthy relationships, communication must act as the centerpiece. All individuals in all relationships whether in marriage or workplace must maintain good communication and check in regularly. Marriages consist of more than just keeping a household, parenting and taking care of bills. With time, the couple begins to understand that the fairy tale- happily ever after has many holes and it takes a lot of effort from both sides to make it work.

In real life, knights on horses rarely ride in and rescue damsels in distress to a happily ever after situation. Consequently, it is important for spouses to remember to talk to one another rather than at each other. Married Couples are in a full-time job called marriage where they should always love and appreciate each other to achieve their marriage goals. The difficult part is that most of the spouses in marriages do not know how to alter their mentality to accommodate real life things that make marriages work. That is why when many couples have difficulties communicating; they focus on the divorce statistics and the number of maintenance cases in the courts. When the spouses realize that the number of cases is too high, they get into panic mode and set the same expectations for their own homes. This expectations and standards tend to kill the marriages that would otherwise thrive.

It is wrong for people to use what is happening around them to gauge their marriages. Most of the statists given to the public only involve detrimental unions. They hardly tell people of the winning marriages and how they got there. In other words, those offering statistics to the public do not tell them what it takes for the marriages to fail or succeed. They fail to discuss the satisfaction levels and communication in marriages, and therefore people do not realize that most marriages fail because of things that would be solved through communication.

Every couple has one thing that they try to avoid conversing about therefore they dance around the matter to avoid conflict. It could be love, sex, or money, but in every relationship, there is that one thing that causes disagreements, and because of the conflicting nature, couples opt not to put the matter to rest. For example, one spouse could want to save money while the other one wants to spend, one wants more sex, while the other one is happy about the current situation et cetera. This results in more conflict.

Arguing in marriages
Communication plays a vital role in any relationship, and it is one of the main pillars of marriage. Arguments and disagreements are also a part of healthy relationships but the success of failure if the differences lie in how the two parties engage each other to settle things.

Couples should understand that arguing is not always unhealthy. It is better than staying silent because lack of communication leads to assumptions, confusion, dissatisfaction, and more misunderstandings. When arguments are done constructively, they help the couple grow. Every spouse should strive to find out more about what their partner wants and thinks. There are many ways of disagreeing healthily and be sure that two people cannot always be in synch. IF a couple is always on the same page in all matters, then one person is faking or ignoring their personal feelings for the sake of the other. In the long term, this setting aside of feelings for the sake of the other person will lead to intense conflicts. Every spouse should look out for the signs that the other person is ignoring their feelings and help them reason together without hiding matters.

When a couple sets aside the blame games and assesses their issues and troubles from a wider perspective, they will easily identify where their different desires overlap. Once the individuals have identified where the opinions overlap, they can come up with agreements. Identifying the point where two people overlap helps them solve the matters faster that when each of them was set on individually. The couple should be affirmative and specific with their agreements to ensure that both parties are on board and that they understand their next step.

CONCLUSION

Thank you for making it to the end of the book *Communication for Couples*: Discover how to *hear Your Partner to Achieve a Healthy Relationship, Improve Mindful Habits, and Grow Empathy for Each Other.* Let us hope that it was informative and that it provided you with all the tools you need to meet your goals irrespective of what they may be. Just because you have finished reading the book does not mean that there is nothing else to learn about the topic. Expanding your horizons is the only way that you can master what you have learned.

The next step is to stop reading and get started with doing what is required of you to ensure that those who depend on you are well taken care of. Put what you have learned into consideration and teach your friends the techniques you have acquired herein. If you find that you need to clarify some things in the book, feel free to read again and do some more research on the topic. Take responsibility for your actions and follow some of the tips you have gathered to improve your relationship with your partner.

Remember, communication keeps connections alive. Make it a habit to compliment your partner; keep the intimacy alive, keep the communication open, look for soft emotions, and rekindle that spark. It's about the two of you; therefore, do not seek to control every outcome in conversations and other sectors of life. Assuming that you do not want to get a divorce, do not threaten your spouse with one. In marriages, people get tempted to make threats of divorce during arguments. Do not! Use the tips in this book to pass your message efficiently.

Do not forget to download other series of books: *Communication Skills for Couples*, *Effective Communication*, and *Communication Skills Training*. All books form one bundle. I am sure you will enjoy the other series of books too.

SOURCES OF INFORMATION

https://healthypsych.com/18-communication-tips-for-couples/

https://www.loveisrespect.org/healthy-relationships/communicate-better/

https://www.psychalive.org/top-10-effective-communication-techniques-couples/

https://psychcentral.com/lib/5-communication-pitfalls-and-pointers-for-couples/

COMMUNICATION SKILLS FOR COUPLES:

21 Practices: Work with your Partner to Build a Mindful Relationship, Improve Emotional Intelligence and Grow Empathy for Each Other (7 Day Challenge Inside)

INTRODUCTION

Congratulations on downloading this book and thank you for doing so.

Healthy, happy relationships and happy endings are not something that's reserved only for the movies. Relationships are challenging, they are hard work and sometimes it may feel like a struggle to even try to understand your other half. But couples who love each other are committed to one thing - *putting in the effort to constantly improve the quality and happiness of their relationship.*

These couples have learned that being in a happy, healthy relationship is completely possible because they realize that effective communication skills are the key to deepening their bond and connection with each other. Couples who have been married for years use several communication skills to successfully understand each other.

The big question is, why do communication skills play such a profound and important role in the success of romantic relationships?

Communication is how couples express their love and emotion for each other. All those deep feelings of love that you feel inside you for your significant other, well, the only way they're going to know how you feel is through effective communication. It is more than just the verbal words that are uttered, it is about the nonverbal communication that takes place too. Since effective communication skills are the foundation upon which healthy, long-lasting romantic relationships are built, it is important for couples to master the 21- techniques needed to improve this aspect, which is what has brought you to this guidebook.

By the time you reach the end of this guidebook, you will be able to build a more mindful relationship, improve emotional intelligence, grow your empathy for each other and finally, improve your communication skills as a couple through the 7-day workshop exercises included in the final chapter.

There are plenty of books on this subject on the market, thanks again for choosing this one! Every effort was made to ensure it is full of as much useful information as possible, please enjoy!

CHAPTER 1: SKILL #1 - ABANDONING YOUR EGO

A loving relationship. That's what we all want. That's what we all desire.

But anyone who has ever been - or is currently- in a relationship will tell you that happy, loving, and healthy relationships are not something that happens just like that. It takes hard work and for both parties to be equally invested and committed enough to put in the effort to *want to build* this relationship.

According to psychologist K. Daniel O'Leary back in 2012 when he and his research team conducted a study into long-term marriages, what was interesting was that happy couples were the ones who both endorsed and expressed the positive feelings that they had for their partners or spouses. The study revealed that 40% of the couples who have been married for more than 10 years affirmed that they were still very much in love. How do they do it?

There's No Room for Ego in a Happy Relationship

The key findings of O'Leary's study were one very simple habit that these couples were doing - *they were focused on the positive feelings,* and they had no problem expressing or reaffirming these feelings about their partner. Positive feelings is the major difference, and therein lies the difference between couples who are happy long term, and couples who struggle to hold onto happiness and a lasting relationship.

An example of how negativity can affect your relationships is when we let ego and pride get in the way and cloud our judgment. Everyone has ego. We all have some level of ego and pride within us, and how clearly these traits get displayed depends on how well we can control them. The ego which is left unchecked can often cause tremendous havoc in a person's life, especially in the relationships which are closest to them. That's because ego is a negative emotion which causes feelings of resentment, anger, fear, and jealousy.

Ego can be a very powerful force that resides within all of us. The term egotistical love exists for a reason, and this isn't the good kind of relationship either. If we let our egos make the decisions instead of our hearts, that's where a lot of problems start to happen. When you let ego take the driver seat, it can cause you to manipulate your relationships, and be the main reason for a lot of arguments, fights, depressions, aggression, passive-aggressiveness, revenge, self-doubt, distrust, intolerance, blame, competition, putting down your partner, and even disrespectful gestures. All of these negative qualities will eventually cause your relationship to deteriorate and breakdown over time. It is an obstacle which prevents effective communication from taking place, and *that is why* it should have no room in your relationship from this point on.

Signs Your Ego Is Damaging Your Relationship

If you're wondering whether ego is playing a part in preventing effective communication from taking place with your partner, take a look at the following signs:

- You're constantly blaming your partner for everything, without taking any responsibility for your actions. It is always someone else's fault.
- You find yourself playing the "victim card" far too often in your relationship.
- You get jealous easily, which leads to a lot of arguments and blame. Jealousy tends to cause a lot of drama within your relationships and causing a lot of toxic energy to manifest itself.
- You fear being rejected by your partner, especially when they seem to be achieving more than you do.
- You feel the need to have the last word all the time, in every argument especially. It is always about you and your opinions, and you don't spend enough time thinking about how your partner feels or what they have to say.

Kicking Ego Out the Front Door Once and for All

If you're reading this book, then you know communication skills is something that you need to work on to improve your relationships. If ego has been a force that you've been dealing with until this point, then there's only one thing left for you to do - kick it out the front door where it belongs.

Ego does not belong in your relationship. It never has, and it never will. To get rid of ego once and for all and start improving communication between you and your significant other, the following strategies are something you need to start working on right now:

- **There's No Need to Always Be Right -** Sure, being right feels good, but you don't *always* have to be right all the time. It is okay to be wrong every now and again. Yes, it may be hard for you to do in the beginning, but this is something you *must* do if you want to start seeing any kind of improvement in your relationship. No one is perfect, and you shouldn't expect yourself to be perfect. There will be times when you find yourself in the wrong. Instead of becoming defensive, use these situations to learn from what went wrong.
- **You Don't Need to Be Superior -** Do you have this need to always be the one who's in charge? The one who's in control? Do you want to be better than everyone? That's ego at work there again. Instead of trying to compete to be better than everyone else all the time, especially your partner, why not focus on yourself and what *you can do to become a*

better person overall? That would be the healthier approach not just for your relationships, but for your everyday life too.

- **Give Up Being Easily Offended -** If you find yourself getting offended far too easily, even over the simplest things, that's ego working behind the scenes again. People are not out to offend you on purpose, especially your partner, so it's time to start practicing a little bit more tolerance. Make it a conscious practice, and remind yourself that everyone expresses themselves differently. When you practice tolerance, it makes it easier to have effective conversations with your partner that don't escalate into arguments.

- **Be Forgiving -** Gandhi once said that *"forgiveness is something that is attributed to the strong".* He was right. Forgiveness is one of the most powerful tools you could possess to make letting go of your ego easier. Not only will you eventually gain the ability to forgive others over time when you let go of your ego, but you'll also learn to forgive yourself. You'll learn acceptance, and you'll learn how to be much happier when you let go of all the anger that resides within you.

CHAPTER 2: SKILL #2 - HOW TO BUILD HEALTHY HABITS AS A COUPLE

How many times have you looked on with envy at other happy couples whom you know? Or even the happy couples that you randomly see around you gazing lovingly into each other's eyes or holding hands as they stroll through the park? They seem almost picture perfect, don't they? But of course, every relationship comes with its own challenges. These happy couples have just found a way to work through those challenges together by communicating well and relying on each other for support. That's the secret to their success.

Now, working on building a lasting relationship is not going to be easy. You can't just enter into a relationship and hope for the best - or that your problems are going to sort themselves out. In fact, the Public Discourse published an article in 2015 which revealed that at least 40-50% of marriages tend to end in divorce. Researchers who spend their time analyzing relationships have always been motivated to find the qualities and traits which contribute to the happiness of a relationship, and one of these factors is to start building happy relationships as a couple.

Healthy Habits That Happy Couples Engage In

Building a happy, healthy relationship starts with building healthy habits together as a couple. Which is why this is Skill #2 that you're about to learn. Why do we need to actively work on building healthy habits? Because in a 2013 *Journal of Social and Personal Relationships* publication by Ogolsky and Bowers, research supported the idea that those who put in the effort to work on their relationships were the ones who managed to cultivate relationships with lasting happiness.

There are healthy habits which happy couples regularly engage in, and here are some practices you can begin applying in your own relationship to improve how you communicate with your partner or spouse:

- **Always Express Your Appreciation -** Do it all day, every day because you can never express appreciation enough. It is always better that your partner feels the extra love and appreciation that you feel for them instead of feeling underappreciated. Love the little things that they do? Let them know! You don't have to do anything elaborate, just simple little gestures, thank you notes, even text messages sent throughout the day letting them know how much you appreciate them can make a huge difference in someone's day.

- **Ask, And You Shall Receive -** Another healthy habit that a lot of couples tend to ignore is to just ask for what they want. Don't assume your partner is going to pick up on the little hints or read your mind and know how to anticipate your thoughts. Assumption is where a lot of communication breakdown tends to happen, which then escalates into fights that could have been avoided. If you want your partner to do something, don't be afraid to just *ask* for it.

- **Working on Chores Together -** This is easily one habit that can be done together, so one person doesn't feel the burden of having to upkeep the house all by themselves. In fact, dividing the workload promotes great teamwork and a sense of happiness knowing that you can count on your partner to share in the workload with you. Rotate the chores amongst yourselves, so there's a sense of fairness and balance, and one person is not stuck doing the same thing all the time.

- **The Language of Love -** Gary Chapman is a relationship therapist who pioneered an excellent concept. This concept was called the Five Love Languages, which involved words of affirmation, physical touch, gifts, quality time and acts of service. This is an excellent habit for couples to start working on together, because the Five Love Languages teach you how to give and receive love with awareness, warmth, and love.

- **They Can Move On -** The biggest downfall in any relationship is the inability of one partner to let things go and move on. Sometimes perhaps both partners could have the tendency to hold onto grudges and bring up issues of the past in arguments. It is time to start cultivating the habit of letting this go. When you have a disagreement or an argument about something, work it out, apologize if need be, and then move on. Let that be the end of it. Forget about it and don't bring it up again in future arguments. It can be a difficult habit to start practicing and adopting in the beginning, but it is a habit that is going to make a huge difference in your relationship once you do.

- **Be Respectful Towards Each Other -** Couples that don't respect each other will have a much harder time staying together. Respect is a vital habit towards cultivating the happiness in your relationship that you seek. Each time that you show disrespect towards your partner, you are in a way letting them know that you don't accept them for the way that they are. Remember that your partner is a unique individual, just like you are, and part of being in a relationship is accepting others and valuing them for who they are, not who you expect them to be.

- **Indulge in Common Interests Activities -** Spend some time doing activities together that *both* you and your partner enjoy. There are bound to be some things that you have in common. It could be a hobby, sport or activity that you like to do together, a shared passion over food perhaps, or even a favorite TV show that both of you love. Make it a habit to do these things together as a couple, it can be great for enhancing your communication skills, especially for activities where you need to work together as a team.

- **Hugging Hello and Goodbye -** When you leave for work in the mornings, start making it a habit to hug your partner and tell them you love them before you head out the door (if you're not doing it already). Wish them a great day ahead, give them a kiss and a hug and those little habits can have a tremendous effect on how both of you feel. It's a great way to start the day on a positive note. When you come home from work in the evenings, greet each other again with a hug and a kiss, asking them how their day was and let them know that you missed them. You could even make this habit something that you do each time you leave or come home, even if it is for little things like running errands or going out to catch up with a few friends for a drink.

CHAPTER 3: SKILL #3 - DEVELOPING EMOTIONAL INTELLIGENCE

Emotional intelligence may seem like it is a skill that better belongs in the workplace, but

Emotional intelligence - or EQ - is defined as an individual's capacity to control and regulate their emotions, and the emotions of others. These two traits are then used to better understand how to improve the interpersonal relationships that surround them, and perhaps even control and regulate the emotions of others to a certain extent.

EQ is a concept which was made popular by Daniel Goleman in his book of the same title, *Emotional Intelligence.* In his book, Goleman outlines just how EQ is growing in popularity as people all over the world are beginning to grasp just how important this quality is in contributing to their success. It doesn't matter if that success is in their career or their everyday life, because either way, EQ is going to provide everyone with the foundation that they need to start forging better, more meaningful connections and relationships. It is forging those deeper, more meaningful relationships that is going to be the exact reason why developing your EQ is going to be important for improving communication skills within your relationship.

In Goleman's book, he outlines the five main qualities (or core pillars as he calls them) that everyone with high EQ should possess - *self-awareness, self-regulation, social skills, motivation, and empathy.* To build effective, successful and meaningful relationships, you need to have mastered *all five* core pillars.

Signs That You or Your Partner May Be Lacking Emotional Intelligence

Because people with high levels of EQ have a much better grasp of their emotions and the way they regulate and control their responses, they tend to make much better partners or spouses. They don't fly off the handle for every little thing, they don't let their emotions dictate their actions and responses, and they have the ability to listen and empathize with others. All these qualities are what lead to better communication because it gives them the ability to remain calm in situations where someone with less EQ might completely overreact in ways that could make the situation worse.

There are several signs which might indicate that you (or your partner) may need to work on improving your EQ. The signs that you want to look out for are:

- **Poor Ability to Control Your Emotions -** If you find yourself losing your temper far too often, getting emotionally carried away in situations that have no real cause for it, you need to work on improving your EQ. Especially if you're guilty of the former, because anger can be an extremely disruptive force in any relationship which will cause it to eventually break down and deteriorate over time.

- **You Can't Read Emotions Properly -** A lack of self-awareness about the way others feel is also a sign of poor EQ. When you're unable to assess how the people around you feel, it becomes much harder for you to forge meaningful connections. Not only will you find it hard to relate to others, they too will find it hard to relate to you.

- **You Find It Hard to Maintain Relationships -** Not just romantic relationships, but any kind of relationships. Friendships, relationships with your family, colleagues, even your kids. Without the necessary social skills, empathy, and self-awareness, you're going to find it very hard to maintain any kind of lasting relationship in your life.

- **You Don't React Appropriately -** If you've ever witnessed someone overreacting or being too emotional and thought "well, that's a bit extreme", that's a sign that the person has poor EQ. They are not aware of their actions and they don't know how to regulate their behavior accordingly, which makes it very difficult for them to react the way that they should in any kind of social setting.

- **They Find It Hard to Cope -** Those with low EQ will find it very difficult to cope when any kind of emotion threatens to overwhelm them.

How to Work on Bettering Your Emotional Intelligence

Emotions are a large part of who we are as human beings. There's no escaping it or ignoring it, so why not learn to control it instead for our own benefit? If you've ever been so overwhelmed by your emotions that you reacted in a way which has caused you a lot of regrets later on, you'll understand just why it is so important to develop a high level of EQ.

We have all, at some point, said something out of anger or in the heat of the moment that we immediately regret as soon as the words have left our mouth, especially during arguments with our partner. While we may apologize profusely and sincerely later on, sometimes the hurt doesn't ever truly go away. Once something has been said, it cannot be taken back, no matter how much you want it to be.

Therefore, it makes sense that if you want to work on improving your relationship, especially the communication aspect of it, you need to first work on *your own emotions* and learn how to regulate your actions by working on improving your EQ. The good news is, anyone can develop a greater level of EQ over time and with a lot of practice:

- **You Need to Understand Yourself First -** Before you can begin to understand another, you must first work on developing a deeper understanding of *yourself*. Knowing who you are, why you react the way that you do is the key to begin developing a greater level of self-awareness. Take a step back and assess how you've been reacting to the different situations in your life and relationship this far and ask yourself, *why did I react that way?* Understand your emotional triggers, reflect on your actions, assess your emotions in detail, and do this as often as needed until you finally understand what makes you tick.

- **Naming Your Feelings -** Another great exercise which is going to enhance your self-awareness abilities is to name your feelings. Instead of just generalizing by saying *I am feeling happy,* define that emotion in greater detail. What level of happiness are you feeling? Cheerful? Joyful? Jubilant? Ecstatic? Practice this method, especially during the moments when you're experiencing those emotions intensely. Make a note of what triggered that reaction within you and then take a step back, assess the way you reacted at that moment and think about how you might have reacted better in such a situation.

- **Start Making Empathy a Habit -** It takes two people to make a relationship work, and your partner's feelings and emotions matter just as much as yours do. Being emotionally intelligent means you have to start developing the ability to empathize, to be able to put yourself in your partner's shoes and see things from their perspective. Being able to understand where they're coming from, feeling what they feel, is going to give you a greater ability to connect with them on a much deeper level than you were previously able to do. That is going to do wonders for improving the communication that occurs in your relationship because you're finally able to see things from your partner's point of view.

- **Knowing When to Walk Away -** An emotionally intelligent person will remain calm and collected. They know when to take a time out, and come back to the situation with a better solution. It is easy to let your feelings overwhelm you if you're not careful. As much as you want to resolve a conflict there and then, sometimes the best decision is to just walk away from the situation to clear your head whenever your emotions are starting to get the best of you. That is the intelligent thing to do, and when you're ready and much calmer, come back and revisit the situation again and see how you can resolve it much better this time.

CHAPTER 4: SKILL #4 - DEVELOPING EMPATHY LISTENING

Well done on making it to skill #4! Hopefully, you've been practicing everything that was learned so far up to this point. Once you have successfully improved your EQ levels, you are now ready to dive a little deeper into the *empathy* portion of it by developing your empathic listening skills.

What Is Empathy Listening?

Essentially, empathy listening involves your ability to *genuinely listen* to what your partner is telling you. You listen sincerely with respect and understanding towards their ideas, values, and opinions. Being able to empathically listen allows you to be on the same page with them, and it is even going to help you on the emotional intelligence front when you need to start tapping into the empathy portion of it.

In a relationship, there is nothing more frustrating for your partner than to feel like they are not being heard. It works both ways too, because imagine if you were trying to express your needs and the way that you're feeling to your partner only to feel like they're not fully understanding what you're trying to communicate. You would feel frustrated too if you were put in that same spot.

Your partner needs to feel like they can come to you, open up and share their innermost feelings and have a conversation with you without the fear of being judged or ridiculed. They need to trust enough that their ideas and opinions are not going to be dismissed, or that you're not going to get defensive over something that's been said. In other words, empathy listening is creating that sense of security for your partner so that they know they can come to you about *anything* at all.

Why Empathy Listening Can Help Communication In a Relationship

Communication works both ways, and both people have to be equally invested in the conversation that's happening for the communication process to be considered effective. Empathy listening is going to be the skill that is going to help you bridge the gap and bring you even closer together with your partner. When they trust you enough and feel comfortable enough to have any kind of conversation with you, even the difficult ones, it can bring the two of you closer together.

Being an empathic listener for your partner doesn't mean that you necessarily have to agree with everything they are saying. Not at all. In fact, it is okay to have different opinions, but when empathy listening is involved, those difference of opinions have a much better chance of becoming healthy discussions rather than heated arguments. An example of when empathy listening is taking place is when you are able to respond "*I hear what you're *saying and I understand why you feel that way, however....."* That's how a healthy discussion should be, and that's the kind of communication two people in a relationship should strive to achieve. If every couple practiced a little more empathy listening, there would be far less heated arguments in the world.

How to Develop Empathy Listening

We may not all be born with high levels of emotional intelligence, or a natural ability to be an empathic listener, but we *can learn to develop* these skills over time. And these are skills that you should work on developing too because they can lead to a much happier, more fulfilling life if everyone could have more empathy and try to connect better with the people around them. It isn't just going to help you in your romantic relationships, it is going to help you in *every* relationship you have in your life. When people start to see you as someone they can turn to, someone they can count on when they need someone to talk to, the connection between you and them starts to deepen and develop into something much more meaningful.

Developing your empathy listening skills is much easier than you think too.

- **It's About Them, Not You -** The first thing that you need to work on to start developing your empathy listening skills is to remember that it's *not about you, it's about them.* It is always about them when someone is trying to have a meaningful conversation with you. This is the time for you to put your needs above others. It can be a challenge to put your personal feelings and opinions aside for a few minutes but remind yourself that this is someone you love that's coming to talk to you. If you love them, then it's time to make it all about them for the next few minutes.

- **No Distractions -** The minute your partner comes to you and says they want to have a conversation, put away all distractions so you can focus on them for the next few minutes. Put your phone away, put your computer away, turn off the TV, anything that's going to pose a distraction, put it away. For the next few minutes, your only point of focus is going to be your partner and listening to what they need.

- **Listening Actively -** There's a very big difference between listening, and listening *actively*. You could be listening and nodding along, saying all the right things, but your mind is actually a million miles away or thinking about something else. That's not active listening. Active listening is when you take in everything that your partner is saving, process it and stay engaged throughout the entire conversation. You know exactly what to say, when to say it and how to say it because you have been paying attention. *That* is active listening.

- **Not Responding with Criticism -** With empathy listening, ideally you want to let your partner be the one who is doing all the talking. It is their time to talk. However, if they were to ask what you think or what you would suggest at some points during the conversation, then your job here is to not respond critically or judgmentally. Empathy listening is about making your partner feel supported, about letting them know that you can see things from their perspective, and you understand why they feel the way that they do. Don't ridicule, judge or criticize them for their opinions because remember, it is all about them this time.

- **Avoid Unsolicited Advice -** Sometimes your partner just needs you to listen to them and that is it. They need someone they can vent their feelings and frustrations to instead of keeping it bottled up inside. Your job, as the supportive partner, is to be what they need and avoid offering unsolicited advice. It can be very off-putting, even to your partner, when that happens, especially when you start telling them what you think they should, or should not do. Unless they specifically ask you for your opinion, remember that empathy listening is all you need to do right now.

CHAPTER 5: SKILL #5 - DON'T BE AFRAID TO SHOW WEAKNESS

In a loving, healthy and happy relationship, you shouldn't have to hide who you are. You should feel so comfortable that you don't feel the need to pretend to be someone that you are not. That special connection between two people is what makes life meaningful. In fact, it is hardwired within our brains to *want* to have these connections with the people who are in our lives. Families, communities, friendships, work, romantic relationships, these connections are all forged because there is something within us that wants to feel that closeness to another human being.

Why Being Vulnerable Can be a Good Thing for Your Relationship

Putting on a brave face all the time can be exhausting, both mentally and physically. Somewhere along the way we live, we somehow developed the belief that showing our vulnerable side is perceived as a sign of weakness - that if we show our vulnerable side, people might take advantage of it or worse, we open ourselves up to being hurt. In an attempt to protect our fragile hearts and shield ourselves from hurt, we have become afraid to show any sign of weakness.

Unfortunately, while your intentions may be good, closing yourself off in this way can also prevent you from connecting with your partner on an intimate level. You need to show your vulnerable side because as terrifying and scary as it is, you *need to know* that you can count on your partner in the moments when you need it the most. Being in a relationship means pain is sometimes unavoidable, but closing this part of yourself off completely from your partner is not the way to deal with it either.

How to Work On Being Less Afraid

It's going to take a while for you to be comfortable showing weakness. It is never easy, to open yourself up to the possibility of being hurt, but if you want to improve communication with your partner - *to be able to have open and honest discussions* - you need to able to talk about anything.

To start accepting that it is okay to show weakness in front of your partner is a process that needs to be worked through in the following stages:

- **Stage 1: Why Are You Reluctant to Show Weakness?** - Have you ever stopped to ask yourself why you feel reluctant to show any sign of weakness? Why do you struggle to reveal the most difficult parts of yourself, and why do you hesitate to open up to your partner? You need to get down to the root cause about what makes this process so difficult for you before you can begin moving onto the second point below.

Pinpointing the root cause of the problem is how you begin to understand yourself on a deeper level, and when you do, you can then slowly open up and explain to your partner just exactly how you feel because you have a much better understanding of yourself too.

- **Stage 2: Working Through Your Emotions -** Only when you have pinpointed the root cause of what makes it difficult for you to open up to your partner can you then begin sorting through your emotions. If you don't work through your own emotions first, you're going to find having difficult conversations with your partner even more of a challenge. You will always struggle to find the right words, and struggle to put your *feelings into words* because you can't manage to work through your own emotions, let alone someone else's.

- **Stage 3: Baby Steps -** Exposing your vulnerable side is going to be a challenge, especially if you (or your partner) has spent all the time trying to do the very opposite by shutting yourself off from these emotions. That's okay, you've already done good so far by first trying to pinpoint why you feel the way that you do, and then trying to work through your emotions. You don't have to rush through the entire process. In fact, taking baby steps is one of the best things you can do for yourself in this situation as you gradually start to get comfortable. You need to be able to trust that your partner is not going to hurt you, and that is going to take a lot of strength to do. If your partner is the one who is afraid to show weakness, help them work through these stages and do it together with them. Treat it like a trust-building exercise that the two of you can work through.

- **Stage 4: Practice Makes Perfect -** It may sound weird to have to "practice" being vulnerable, but this is going to help you learn to trust your partner over time. Take it slow, and maybe once a week, sit down with your partner and talk about one weakness that you would normally otherwise try to hide. Tell them how you feel, why you feel this way, and how they could support you in making you feel comfortable about expressing this weakness moving forward. Practicing being vulnerable is merely a simple exercise of being able to talk about what you perceive as a "weakness" and being able to answer honestly if your partner has any questions about it. Working through this stage together and communicating as a couple is a great way to strengthen your bond, especially when you see that your partner is going to support you through it.

- **Stage 5: Being Honest -** This is a very important stage. This is where you're going to have to fight all your natural instincts to hide your true emotions by responding with the usual "*I'm fine"* phrase. If you're not feeling fine, then tell your partner. Let them in instead of shutting them out. If there is something that they can do to help you feel better, to feel safer, to feel more accepted, let them know. Let them in on this journey with you, they can only help you and support you the way that you need if they can understand what you're going through.

- **Stage 6: Creating Your Safe Space -** Sometimes it helps to create a safe space where you can have these difficult and intimate discussions with your partner. Creating a safe space within your home, where the two of you can sit down and communicate about this is essential for creating the right frame of mind and the right environment for a conducive, healthy discussion. Talking about this in a situation where you or your partner might be distracted, agitated, anxious, or maybe even just not in a good mood at the moment is going to make it harder for a meaningful conversation to take place. You're opening up to your partner about the things that worry about the most, and this is a very important talk which must be done at the right time and in the right place.

CHAPTER 6: SKILL #6 – UNDERSTANDING BODY LANGUAGE

Did you know that 55% of our communication is demonstrated through our body language? This was certainly a very interesting revelation by the author of *Silent Messages*, Dr. Albert Mehrabian. According to Dr. Mehrabian, only 7% of our communication occurs through the use of words, and that, compared to body language, is a very small percentage. It, therefore, goes without saying that body language plays a very important, if not crucial role, in being able to effectively communicate in relationships.

If you are correctly able to read someone's body language, you've already got incredible leverage on your hands right now. It is this very skill that is going to help you deduce how a person truly feels without them having to ever say a word, especially if this person is your partner. By being able to read these signals, you'll be able to anticipate their needs much better and support them in ways they may not even realize that they want at the time. A lot of body language occurs on a subconscious level, without us even realizing it. Our words may say that we're fine, but our bodies are telling a completely different story altogether.

Basic Cues to Reading Your Partner's Body Language Correctly

In a relationship, your partner may be displaying a wide array of body language signals that signify what's on their mind or how they may be feeling at that time. Communicating effectively with your partner in any situation is going to depend heavily on your ability to read the signals that they are giving off, and better understand their moods so you will be able to adjust and moderate your responses and reaction to better suit the situation.

Body language can be complex, but at the same time, extremely fascinating. It is like unlocking clues to a puzzle, where the more you understand, the greater your awareness will be. In this case, the puzzle is your partner and what you're trying to do is understand how they feel without them having to tell you. Body language can give you clues into the feelings that they may not want to reveal, and when used correctly, can rapidly change the way that you and your partner communicate.

You don't have to be an expert to start picking up on the little body language nuances that your partner may be exhibiting. In fact, some clues are just a matter of paying attention and noticing the little things. That alone is going to make all the difference in the world in the way that you communicate and anticipate their needs.

- **Facial Expressions -** This is where most of the body language signals are going to emit from - the facial expressions. Anything from the eyes, the lips, mouth, or even the way that they tilt their head is going to mean something. If your partner lifts their eyebrows, for example, this could signal skepticism, surprise or discomfort. If their mouth and lips are pursed in a thin line, it could mean that they are unhappy, irritated or angry. The clenching of the jaw which might happen during an argument could signal to you that they are stressed or angry.

- **Eye Contact -** Another big one you want to look out for is eye contact. If, during a conversation, you notice that your partner's eyes are unfocused or looking behind you, for example, it could mean that they are preoccupied, distracted, anxious or maybe just not that interested in the conversation. Eye contact is another way of detecting when someone may or may not be telling the truth. According to several body language experts, whenever a person is telling a lie, they tend to look towards the left. They also struggle to maintain consistent eye contact the way a person would do if they were being honest. If you're trying to suss out whether your partner may be lying to you or not, look for these indicators and see how well they manage to maintain eye contact.

- **The Arms and the Hands -** The arms and hand gestures are a bit of a tricky one because they could hold several different meanings. Crossing arms in front of the chest, for example, doesn't necessarily mean that your partner is closed off to the conversation or shutting you out. They could be doing this out of habit, because it's a comfortable position, or maybe because they happen to feel cold. You'll need to observe the context in which this gesture is occurring. If your partner crosses their arms in front of their chest halfway during a disagreement, for example, it means they are being defensive. On the other hand, if you notice that your partner has their palms facing up and outwards during a conversation, this is a good sign because it means they are relaxed, honest and sincere. If your partner clenches their fists, it could be a signal that they're feeling angry or tense.

- **The Proximity -** How close someone chooses to be next to you is a signal about how they feel about you. If your partner chooses to stand close to you in a relaxed, comfortable manner, they are happy and comfortable being around you and being in your presence. If they move away from you however, it means the opposite.

- **Fidgeting About -** Any fidgeting, either while sitting, is a sign that your partner may be feeling irritated, bored or anxious. This is applicable too if they fiddle with their hands, or even objects in their hands. If you're about to have a serious conversation with them and you notice all these signs beforehand, you might want to think about postponing the talk to another time when they are much calmer. Ask them what's wrong when you see these signs at work and encourage them to talk about it, especially if they are feeling particularly nervous or anxious.

Other general signs of body language that you might often see happening in your relationship with your partner include:

- **Brow Rubbing:** An indication they could be worried or doubtful.
- **Head Scratching:** An indication they could be deep in thought or trying to solve a problem. Sometimes used to indicate confusion too.
- **Nose Touching:** Generally associated with being an indication that a person is lying. If casually done, it could be an indication that they may feel pressured about something.
- **Ear Rubbing:** Specifically, rubbing behind the ears. This is an indication your partner is afraid of being misunderstood, or they are afraid they're not going to understand.
- **Finger Pointing:** An indication that they could be feeling authoritative. Also sometimes an indication of aggressive or angry emotions.

How Does Your Partner Behave During an Argument?

During a disagreement, you may be so wrapped up in having your say and focused on your own feelings that you forget to think about how your partner feels in this situation. But paying attention to body language is exactly what you need to be thinking about too because reading the signs is exactly what's going to help you diffuse the situation much faster. When you notice the following signs which signal disapproval, feelings of aggression or anger, it's time to take a step back and start to approach the argument differently:

- Nostrils flared
- Teeth bared
- Sneering
- Arms crossed tightly in an angry manner across the chest
- Frown between the eyes
- The body turned to point away from you
- Pointing or jabbing you
- Clenched fists
- Invading your personal space
- Posture is stiff and rigid
- Contracted pupils

- Rapid body movements
- Rubbing the back of the neck

CHAPTER 7: SKILL #7 – LEARNING TO TALK ABOUT IT

Having difficult conversations can be, well, difficult. Unfortunately, as much as we would like to avoid having these discussions, it is not always possible. In any relationship, there is going to come a time where you're going to have these difficult conversations, especially in a romantic relationship where you're sharing so much of your life with another individual.

Why You Need to Learn to Talk About It

Because you can't avoid problems and issues forever. There is no "wishing it would go away" or sweeping it under the rug and pretending like it doesn't exist. That's not a healthy relationship, and it won't be a recipe for a long-lasting relationship either. No, whether you like it or not, you need to learn to talk about it.

The more you ignore your problems, the harder they will be to fix. In a scenario where your partner may want to talk about and address these issues but you don't, it can cause a lot of frustration, tension, and resentment over time. Your partner will get frustrated eventually over your refusal to talk things about, and eventually, it will cause your relationship to break down, possibly even end, if your partner feels like they are getting nowhere with you.

Relationships are not easy, and conflict is something that comes along with the package. While conflict and the issues that arise are sometimes beyond your control, what you *do have control* over is how you handle and manage the situation.

Start Learning How to Talk About It

If you're worried that talking about it could lead to potential arguments, don't be. Just because it is a difficult conversation, it doesn't mean that there can only be one outcome - or that it has to end badly in a heated debate between you and your partner. You have the power to control your outcome when you learn how to talk about it by following these strategies:

- **Understand Your Why -** Before you even begin, it is important that you understand *why* you're learning to talk about things. You may not like it and you may not even want it, but this is something that you're going to have to do regardless. *Why?* Because that's what healthy relationships are about. It is not about living in denial, ignoring the problem and hoping it is going to resolve itself. No, to have a relationship that is both happy and healthy, you *must* be able to talk about anything, both good and bad.

- **Remaining Calm -** The ability to stay calm is going to be your biggest asset in determining a positive outcome for any conversation that you have, especially the difficult ones. This is where the emotional intelligence and empathy listening skill is going to be extremely beneficial to you. During a conversation that is particularly difficult, you can sometimes struggle to maintain your composure or to keep your voice calm and friendly. When your voice starts to escalate, your partner is likely going to follow because they will sense all that nervous and tense energy that is happening and find it hard to keep their emotions in check too. Whenever you feel yourself start to get more emotional, press pause on the conversation, explain to your partner why you're doing so, and then suggest that the two of you take a 10 to 15-minute break before revisiting this issue again when you're both much calmer.

- **Use Positive Language -** Learning to talk about the things that are difficult can be much easier if both you and your partner adopt the approach to only use positive language during the conversation. Phrases such as *I hear what you're saying and I value what you have to say* or *I know this is difficult to talk about, but I'm here to support you and we can work through this together* are examples of some great positive language that can be used to help control the conversation and steer it in the right direction. It minimizes the chances of things escalating and getting out of hand.

- **Stay Relevant -** Another important aspect of learning how to talk about difficult matters is to remember to remain relevant. Talk about the situation or issue that is currently happening, and avoid bringing up past arguments to support your case. This will only serve to either hurt your partner's feelings by reminding them that you haven't forgotten or let go of what's happened in the past, or it could make them defensive and shut them off to the conversation completely. There is no need to rehash old arguments, in fact, Skill #1 is what you need to bring into play right now and abandon your ego. Leave it outside where it belongs.

- **Manage Your Expectations -** If you start a conversation with your partner with a mindset that this is going to go badly, then that's all you're going to be thinking about and guess what? You'll probably sabotage the conversation and make it worse without even realizing it. Why? Because you *expected it.* Learning to talk about difficult topics with your partner can be hard, but going into it with a negative mindset is only going to make it harder for both of you to achieve a fruitful discussion. Instead, keep an open mind about it. You might just be surprised at the outcome.

- **Pick the Right Time -** With difficult conversations, timing is everything. You need to pick the right time, place and be in the right frame of mind to have this conversation. Not just you, but your partner too. The best time to talk about what you and your partner may find difficult is when you're both feeling calm, relaxed and in an environment where the two of you feel safe and happy. It is best that the environment is free from distractions too, so both of you can focus on the conversation at hand. Choosing to talk about it when someone is doing the dishes, watching television, or just returned from a stressful day, for example, is *not the right time* to have a difficult conversation.

- **Be Respectful -** A lot of couples prefer not to talk about things because they don't want to risk an argument. In the heat of the moment, words get thrown out and often, these may be words that we later come to regret. It's perfectly understandable to feel this way, and what's going to help you during this situation is to remember to always be respectful towards your partner. After all, this is someone that you love, someone you care for deeply and you would never want to hurt them under any circumstances. Let your partner know before you begin that you're about to talk about something which you find difficult so that they are on board with what's happening.

CHAPTER 8: SKILL #8 – DIGITALLY DISCONNECTING

Does your partner complain that you're on the phone far too much? Or perhaps it happens far too often where you want some quality time with your partner, only to find that they're not 100% present with you because they're too preoccupied with scrolling through social media?

The digital world we live in today is great, but it has also created several problems in the process. One of these problems is interrupting quality time which could be invested in romantic relationships instead. Brigham Young University conducted a study into this very subject, investigating to what extent technology in interfering and how damaging it can be to romance. The conclusion of that study was not only did technology hurt your relationship, it could affect your psychological health too. Specifically, the term "technoference" was used in this study and it discovered that the higher the technoference, the more conflict and relationship dissatisfaction you're likely to experience.

Why We Need to Step Away from Technology

Relationships, as we know it today, are very different from what they were a decade ago. The introduction of smartphones and social media has rapidly changed the way we connect with the world and the people around us. As our mobile devices offer greater features, our addiction to them seems to grow in equal measure. All you have to do is observe on your next train or bus commute home just how many people are glued to their devices throughout the journey.

The statistics revealed by Pew Research Centre showed that a whopping 67% of people often checked their devices even if it didn't ring, while 44% of people slept with their phones next to them. And then, there's 29% of those surveyed who said they simply "couldn't live" without their mobile devices. It is safe to say that most relationships in the 21st century have a constant "third party" in them in the form of digital devices.

While mobile phones have done our lives a world of good and made connecting with people no matter where they are in the world, when it comes to *real life connections,* we need to step away from our digital devices in order to connect with the person who is right next to us instead of on a screen. It is important to digitally disconnect when spending quality time with your partner because when you're distracted by what's happening on your phone, you're missing out on crucial moments, important information and body language signals which your partner may be trying to convey about what they're feeling.

When you disconnect from what's digital, you're able to connect to the physical. Being present and engaged in your relationship and your surroundings is what your relationship needs, not another social media tweet,

Instagram post or Facebook update. A healthy relationship needs communication that is happening in real life, not over text messages. In fact, more fights tend to happen over text message miscommunication than if you were to have an actual conversation, because of how quickly and easily messages can be misread or misinterpreted. Don't use text messages to apologize over disagreements, or to argue with your partner. Do it in person because that essential human connection is what is needed to strengthen your relationship. The more dependent you are on technology, the more disconnected from your partner you will feel over time.

Technology has also made it possible for many of us to work remotely, even when we're away from the office. Responding to emails, following up with clients, organizing meetings, it has now become possible for us to bring work with us everywhere we go. Sometimes, this can prove to be a convenience, but other times it just makes it that much more difficult for us to achieve work-life balance, especially when it takes time away from your partner because you can't be present with them when your mind is focused on work instead. It makes you wonder whether being connected digitally all the time is really such a good thing for any of us.

How to Disconnect Digitally and Start Being Engaged Physically in Your Relationship

You don't need a big romantic gesture or a fancy, overpriced dinner to show your partner that you love them. You could show just how much they mean to you without ever spending a cent, all you need to do is simply spend more time with them. Give them your full attention and for those few moments that you spend together, make a commitment to be there and be present. Everything else can wait for a moment.

Here's how you can start digitally disconnecting from your devices to improve your communication as a couple:

- **Set Expectations -** Understandably, disconnecting for an entire day or maybe two is not entirely possible for many couples. The key is to find a middle ground that works for both of you by setting expectations. Start by committing to setting aside one hour each day to spend time with each other without your phones, tablets or computers present. Both partners need to come to an agreement to commit to spending this quality time together, and as it becomes a habit, you can slowly move onto increasing the amount of time spent, provided you're both in agreement with it.

- **Set Tech-Free Zones -** Set up some zones around the home which are "tech-free". The bedroom for example, or the family room, maybe even the dining room during meal times could be set up as spaces where you're not going to use technology during the times that you're there. This allows you to focus instead of having conversations with your partner instead of constantly checking for the next email or social media update. This could be great for improving your sleep patterns too.

- **Turn It Off -** Putting your phone aside or putting it on silent alone is not going to be enough. That's not digitally disconnecting, because as soon as you hear it vibrating, your attention is going to be immediately drawn towards your phone, wondering what alert or update you just received. No, you need to *turn it off* completely. No ifs, no buts. Off.

- **Do Activities Together Which Don't Involve Your Phones** – A great way to get your mind off your phone is to have it focused on something else. At least a few times in a week, do an activity with your partner and throughout the duration of that activity, make it a commitment that neither of you is going to check your mobile phones until it's over.

You don't have to completely cut yourself off from the digital world. The key to a happy, healthy relationship is to find that balance so that your relationships don't get neglected along the way. After all, couples from a decade ago managed to survive without these fancy digital devices that we have today. You can do the same.

CHAPTER 9: SKILL #9 – APOLOGIZING MINDFULLY

When you apologize to your partner, how often do you *mean* it? Apologizing and saying all the right words is easy, but apologizing *mindfully* requires that you think about what you're saying and say it with emotion and feeling. Mindful apologies are more meaningful because of the sincerity and genuine feeling that is involved. Anyone can just utter the words *I'm sorry* for the sake of doing so, or because it is expected of them. But is an apology for the sake of doing so *really* an apology at all?

The Purpose of an Apology

An apology is supposed to serve two purposes. The first is to show remorse over your actions, and the second is to acknowledge that your actions may have caused someone else a lot of hurt and pain.

For a healthy relationship to exist, you must learn how to apologize mindfully. Nobody is perfect, and along the way, we are bound to commit mistakes. Yes, mistakes do get made along the way, but the difference lies in the way that you handle what happens after those mistakes have been made, how you restore the harmony and the trust in your relationship, and how you let your partner know that you are genuinely sorry for what happened.

An apology symbolizes your willingness to admit your mistake, and that alone is a step in the right direction. There are many people who simply refuse to admit when they are wrong because they let their pride and ego get in the way. They would rather let their relationship suffer than to have to admit they are wrong. You don't want to be one of these people. When you are willing to admit that you've made a mistake and own up to it, you're giving your partner (or anyone else for that matter) the opportunity to communicate with you so you can start working through your feelings together, to discuss what is acceptable behavior and what isn't moving forward.

Apologies let your partner know that you realize what you did was wrong, and that your behavior may have been unacceptable. An apology lets your partner know that you are ready to work on building and re-establishing that bond in your relationship. It allows the healing process to begin and reassures your partner that you do care about their feelings and you're willing to work on improving your flaws.

What Happens If You Don't Apologize?

Needless to say, one of the biggest consequences of refusing to apologize when you've made a mistake is the deterioration of your relationship. Your partner may be patient and forgiving, but the biggest mistake you could commit is to take that for granted. Everyone has their limits, even the most patient person. One day, when your partner has had enough, they will eventually pack up and leave. You don't want to wait until it gets to that point.

Not apologizing is going to cause a lot of hurt and animosity, tension, stress, and worst of all, emotional pain. Anger can do more damage to a person's soul than you realize, and the words you say cannot be taken back once it has been put out there.

Why Some People Find Apologies So Hard?

We know that apologies are necessary to repair and restore relationships. Yet, so many people struggle to utter these two simple words and to mean what they say. Aside from ego and pride which gets in the way, why are apologies sometimes so difficult?

For one thing, it takes a lot of effort and courage to admit that you were in the wrong. In doing that, you take on the blame and put yourself in a position that is vulnerable, which a lot of people actively want to avoid. Another reason why apologies are so difficult for some people is because they may be ashamed or embarrassed about the way that they behaved. They know what they did or said was wrong, and they are so ashamed of their actions that they can't bring themselves to face it.

And then there's arrogance, which falls right along the same lines as ego and pride does. The only way to overcome this is to let go of your need to always be right and to feel superior. After all, when dealing with someone that you love, do you really feel the need to be better than they are?

How to Start Apologizing Mindfully

Saying *I'm sorry* alone simply isn't enough. An apology is not going to mean anything if you don't put any emotion into it. If you're only going to apologize because it's what you're "supposed to do", then you're better off not apologizing at all.

Apologizing mindfully can open the door to much better communication and healing in the relationship, and here's is how you do it:

- **Don't Just Feel Remorse, Express It -** Put emotion and feeling behind your words when you apologize. With the emotional intelligence skills, you have developed, empathize and put yourself in your partner's shoes. How would you feel if you were in their situation? Being authentic and genuine with your apology requires you to feel the hurt that they could be feeling, and in doing so, feel remorse over having hurt them in that way.

- **Don't Wait to Apologize -** It is also equally important to apologize as soon as you realize that you were in the wrong. Don't wait until tomorrow, next week or next month to do it, because it then loses all meaning. The hurt and the damage has been done, and if you don't do something at that moment to fix it, it might end up being a case of too little too late.

- **Accepting Responsibility -** Empathy is once more going to come into play here as you accept responsibility for what you did wrong. When you realize just how much hurt you've caused your partner or how you've wronged them, let them know that you understand how your actions have made them feel. For example, expressing *I'm sorry, I know I hurt you when I snapped at you in anger. I was wrong, I shouldn't have done that and I am truly sorry.*

- **Forgo the Excuses -** A mindful apology is a sincere apology which comes from the heart. Which means you need to forgo the excuses and attempts at trying to justify your behavior. There are no excuses for hurting the person that you love, and if that happens, you need to accept responsibility for your actions and don't try to shift the blame or make excuses which could only weaken your apology and make it seem less sincere.

CHAPTER 10: SKILL #10 – NO JUDGMENT ZONE

Judgment. It is among the most damaging forces that a relationship could experience, aside from anger. Whenever you judge someone, especially your partner, the message that you're sending them is that you don't accept them for who they are. In turn, the hurt emotions that they experience from your judgment will build up resentment within them and over time, the relationship will fall apart.

Dr. Margaret Paul (Ph.D.), a relationship expert, pointed out that judgment, this subconscious behavior we engage in without even realizing that we're doing it, is something that "erodes intimacy" in a couple's relationship. Regardless if it is whether you judge others, or even if you were judging yourself, Paul points out that judgment causes a lot of problems in a relationship.

Why Judgment Is Such A Damaging Quality

Each time that you judge your partner, you make them feel embarrassed, insecure, perhaps even anxious and tense. When they experience this form of rejection from you, as a way to protect themselves, they will close themselves off to you because they don't feel secure enough to open up freely and be themselves. This is how judgment erodes intimacy.

In a loving relationship, you should not have to hide who you are. When you judge, you're preventing the other person from truly being themselves. Expecting your partner to live up to your expectations - especially if you have high standards - is unrealistic, and a little bit unfair at the same time. Everyone is different, and no two people are going to be the same. Yes, you and your partner may have several things in common which drew you together in the first place, but you are *still* two different people. Expecting them to live up to your expectations and then judging them when they fail to, is unfair.

Mother Teresa once said that if you spend far too much time judging people, then you have no time left to love them. When a relationship is new and exciting, it is easy to fall in love when everything seems to be going perfectly. Everyone always puts their best foot forward and presents their best qualities because they're trying to impress their partner. As the relationship continues to progress, that's when all the other behaviors, traits, and quirky personality elements start to show through. Some you may find endearing, others you may find annoying and it is during this phase that judgmental thoughts start to swim around in your head.

Why Do We Judge the People We Love?

You may not be doing it on purpose. Sometimes you may not even realize you're doing it all. The human brain is wired to judge those who we perceive to be different from ourselves, and when your partner behaves differently in a way that you would, judgment surfaces.

Judgment could be in the form of comparing your partner to other men, your friend's partners, thinking that you know better than them and trying to change them to be more like what you expect them to be. Each time you find yourself judging your partner, take note of the way you feel at that moment. You're likely to feel less connected or close to them as you normally would. Why? Because judgment is creating a separation barrier between the two of you. What's worse is that your partner often may not even realize they are under scrutiny as you silently judge them, and they won't understand why there has been a shift in your emotions or the way that you feel.

How to Stop Judging the People We Love

Now that we know that judgment is a damaging force in any relationship (not just the romantic ones), the next question that we need to ask ourselves is *how do we stop*? You can still save your relationship before it's too late, here's what you need to do to stop judging your partner:

- **Don't Expect Them to Be Like You** - Your partner is doing their best, and giving it their best in your relationship. They're doing the best that they know how, based on their experiences and what they've been through in life so far. Nobody would purposely be on their worst behavior. This is what you need to remind yourself of, and why each time you find yourself about to judge your partner, remember that *they are not like you*. The sooner you let go of that expectation, the quicker you'll be able to learn how to stop judging the one that you say you love.

- **Listen to What They're Saying -** When we often find ourselves judging our partners, we're not listening. You've already mentally blocked yourself off and all you care about at that moment is how *you feel* and what *you think.* This especially happens during an argument, when you disagree with what your partner is saying and you judge them for it. Again, you're going to have to rely on emotional intelligence to get you through this. Empathize, take a step back and try to *actively listen* to what they are telling you and see the truth in what they say. Understand that whatever it is they are telling you, it is how they perceive things from their point of view, and there's nothing wrong with that. Keep an open mind and you will learn how to judge less.

- **You're Not There to Manage Their Life -** Everyone is entitled to live their life the way that they want. A relationship is two people coming together and sharing their lives together, both ups, downs, good and bad. That's the beauty of a relationship, that two people who are so different can come together and blend their lives together. To judge your partner less, sometimes you need to focus less on trying to manage their lives. You're there to love them and support them, not correct their lives and try to micromanage everything to a point that you judge them when they fail to live up to your expectations.

- **Let Go of Expectations -** And of course, you need to let go of your expectations. Nothing is going to be a bigger let down than for you to set high standards that are almost impossible to meet, especially for your partner. They are not obligated to live life according to your rules, and you need to let go of expecting far too much from them. Expect them to be nothing but themselves, and you'll have a much happier relationship at the end of the day.

- **Focus Less On Their Flaws, And More On Their Good Qualities -** Another downfall of the human brain is that we're, again, programmed to focus more on the negative. Which is why it always seems much easier to be negative and see everything that is wrong instead of focusing on the positive. Remaining positive is hard work and requires constant effort. To learn to judge your partner less, start focusing on their good traits instead. Remind yourself of all the reasons you fell in love in the first place. Make this a consistent and conscious effort and over time, you will increase your compassion rather than your judgment.

CHAPTER 11: SKILL #11 – WORKING ON YOURSELF FIRST

This is going to be a very important chapter as you work on your self-improvement. If you want to become an improved version of yourself and improve your romantic relationships, then you don't just need to focus on improving the external aspects, you need to focus on what's within, too. The very reason you picked up this book is that you want to improve the communication that happens between you and your partner to become the better version of yourself for the sake and health of your relationship.

Where to Begin When It Comes to Self-Improvement

It starts with reshaping your mindset. Changing your mindset is an important step if you want to see visible change taking place in your relationship. Lao Tzu once uttered the wise words, *"If you correct your mind, the rest of your life will eventually fall into place."* That sentence alone highlights just how vital it is to reshape your mind; how powerful this one tactic can be.

Developing a positive mindset is something that you need to make a part of your life. A happy, healthy relationship is not just going to fall into your lap, you are going to have to work hard to get there. A shift is all it takes to start seeing things in a brand-new light, which is when meaningful change starts to happen. It is important to begin cultivating a better mindset if you want to improve yourself because:

- **It Will Help to Improve Your Focus** - One of the things you're going to need to work on improving is to minimize the negativity that is going on inside your mind. Yes, we all have it, we're all guilty of the noisy, negative chatter that often holds us back and prevents us from seeing the good in others (or ourselves). When your mind is not as clouded by negativity, you will be able to focus on seeing the good things that are happening in your life and learn to appreciate them more.
- **It Improves Your Self-Esteem** - A healthy self-esteem is what you're after, because in the long-run, it will lead to much higher levels of satisfaction in your everyday life and in your relationship.

Self-Improvement Begins with You

The choice to improve yourself starts right now, at this very moment. You have the choice to improve your life today and here is how you begin reshaping your mindset for the better:

- **Learning to Be More Flexible** - Learning to be flexible is an important step towards building a healthier, more positive way of thinking because if you don't, you will find it difficult and frustrating to overcome bumps in the road when things may not be going your way. You can't control everything, especially when it comes to relationships, and learning to be flexible is how you cope with the ups and downs and challenges that come your way. Being flexible is how you learn to work better together with your partner as a team, the way that it should be.
- **Stop Focusing On Your Failures** - The mistakes of the past have a way of haunting us if we don't find a way to deal with them and let them go. This baggage that we carry with us and bring into the new relationships that we forge are not healthy for either party. Reshaping your mind includes changing the way you see failures because as you work towards improving yourself, you are going to have to overcome a few challenges which may sometimes take a few setbacks and tries before you get it right. Instead of viewing failures as "failures", see them as learning lessons instead and use them as a gauge of what works and what doesn't.
- **Find Something That Inspires You Daily** - Begin cultivating a positive mindset for your self-improvement by focusing on something each day that inspires you. Wake up each morning and make the first thing that you see something that is going to inspire you for the rest of the day, like a positive quote or image for example. It could be something as simple as a quote or saying that stirs up emotions within you, or maybe even images of inspirational individuals you would love to emulate. Put them around your home or at your work station in the office, places where it would be hard to miss so you can constantly be reminded of it.
- **Positive Talk, Positive Thoughts** - Your thoughts have the power to influence you in more ways than you know. To start cultivating and reshaping your mindset towards self-improvement, you need to start pushing out every negative thought about yourself out of your mind and replace with positive

thoughts instead. You're not doing your relationship any good if all you can bring to it is negativity, because it will affect both you and your partner in a bad way. If you're finding it difficult to list down the positive qualities about yourself, turn to your partner for help and get them to list what they think are your most positive attributes. Toss out negativity one day at a time. Always look at the silver lining, train yourself to do it. It can be hard to see how they could help, but positive affirmations do remarkable feats when it comes to shifting a person's perception and mindset. The most successful, prominent individuals - motivational speakers for example - in this world are constantly talking about how positive affirmations can do wonders to change your life. If it works for them, it can work for you too.

- **Remember to Love Yourself -** This is perhaps the most important practical self- improvement tip you can take away with you from this chapter. If you don't love yourself, how do you expect others to love you? Your partner is in a relationship with you right now *because they love you.* If you are going to constantly rely on others to feel worthy, you will never become the improved version of yourself that you long to be. If you can easily list all the things you don't like about yourself at the snap of your finger, you can do the same when it comes to listing the qualities you do love about yourself.

CHAPTER 12: SKILL #12 – USING IRONY TO DIFFUSE UNPLEASANT SITUATIONS

Forging connections to today's modern world isn't as simple as one might expect. We are surrounded by all sorts of technological devices and gadgets which are supposed to bring us closer to the ones we love and the people who matter, yet somehow we seem to be more *disconnected* than ever, and we struggle to form intimate human connections sometimes. Talk about irony, right?

Irony. It works well in some contexts. But is using irony to diffuse an unpleasant situation in a relationship a good thing?

Types of Irony

In general, there are three different categories of irony, which are dramatic, verbal, and situational. Verbal irony is what happens when a person's intention is the exact *opposite* of what they are saying. For example, if you were caught in the middle of a traffic jam, you might say something like "I love how smooth the traffic is!".

Situational irony, on the other hand, is when the outcome of a situation is completely *different* from what you expected it to be. Situational irony is something which is used in a lot of sitcoms. One example of situational irony at play is when you plan an elaborate surprise birthday party for your friend, only to realize that her birthday is *next* month and not on the day that you threw her party on.

And then there is dramatic irony, in which also we see a lot of in movies. This is when you, as the audience, already know something that the character or person in the movie does not. In a horror movie, for example, you know it is a bad idea to go into a dark and deserted room, yet the person in the movie walks into the room anyway only to realize what do you know? Turns out it *was* a bad idea.

In a sitcom or movie situation, irony can bring a few laughs, and even make an unpleasant situation seem funny. Irony is even used in literature quite a bit too, and depending on the context which the author uses it, sometimes it can produce a few laughs in the reader.

In a real-life romantic situation, is irony necessarily the best approach to take? The thing about irony is that it can serve as a defense mechanism for some people's ego. It is used along the similar lines of sarcasm, where we use verbal irony to protect ourselves in a way from getting hurt or embarrassed. These people would rather have others laugh *with* them than *at* them. But if you're going to resort to using irony all the time in a relationship to help diffuse unpleasant situations, your partner might not necessarily see that as a good thing. You could be perceived as not taking the situation seriously enough if you're going to always go around making jokes about it, especially if your partner is trying to have a serious discussion with you.

There are also some people, who resort to irony because they want to avoid conflict. Conflicts tend to make some people uncomfortable, and rather than face the problem head-on, they use irony to try and diffuse the situation instead. Again, using this approach might not always be a good thing in a romantic relationship. If your partner is the serious type who would rather talk things out and resolve the matter then and there, and your approach is to use irony to deal with the situation, that could only end up causing more problems. Your partner may get frustrated at your lack of perceived willingness to resolve the situation, and you will get frustrated too because you're actively trying to avoid conflict and dealing with it in the way that you think is best.

Should We Use Irony in Our Relationships?

Relationships are a complicated system. If your partner has a sense of humor, yes it can certainly be used to help diffuse unpleasant situations, because it helps the two of you to see the funny side of things. Perhaps even get a couple of good laughs or two. But as for whether irony is the *best* approach to take? Well, perhaps not all the time. It can be either a good thing or a bad thing, depending on how you perceive it and how you use it within your relationship.

The thing about relationships is that it involves two people coming together, trying to work together to create harmony. When there's a disagreement over the way things are done, middle ground and compromise must be created so that both parties end up happy and satisfied with the outcome. When you know that in certain situations, using irony might upset your partner even more, so try to meet them halfway and figure out another approach to resolving the unpleasant situation.

Instead of irony, what might be better is to use humor to help relieve the tension that is sometimes felt from time to time. Being able to laugh what brings people closer together, and having a sense of humor has always been recognized as an important quality to have in a long-term relationship. Humor is merely about the funny things that get said, it is also about the things that you do together as a couple. It is about having *fun* in each other's presence, and indulging in activities that make you laugh.

A sense of humor helps you see the happier, lighter side of life and revel in it, and that is what makes it a much better approach to take than irony. We will talk more about humor in the next chapter and what it can do for your relationship.

CHAPTER 13: SKILL 13 – A COUPLE THAT LAUGHS TOGETHER, STAYS TOGETHER

If you could choose what the absolute favorite was, what would it be? Would it be that you laugh together a lot as a couple? Have you experienced that laughter which leaves you in stitches? Cracking up so hard that you can't help the tears from pouring down your cheeks and your sides aching so hard you feel as if you could never stand up again? That kind of laughter is a magical thing that can bring two people together in exceptional ways.

Picture what it would be like for a moment, to be in a relationship that had no laughter. No sense of humor, no shared memories that leave you both smiling and laughing at the very recollection. How would that make you feel?

Laughter has the power to heal and it can touch a deep emotion within us that no other emotion can. Research conducted by the University of North Carolina revealed that couples who shared laughs together had a much happier relationship because of the closeness that they felt and the support they received from their partner.

A lot of times, the challenges that we go through in life boils down to our capacity to handle it, the way we perceive it and the relationships that we have in our lives that help us get through it. The stronger the bond you share with your partner, the better your ability to communicate and work through issues as a couple.

How Laughter Can Benefit Your Romantic Relationship

A couple who laughs together share a much stronger bond, and because of that bond, they are able to overcome challenges and conflicts that crop up in their relationship much better than couples who don't have a bond that is that strong. Many couples have listed a sense of humor as one of the qualities that they look for in a long-term partner, because if you can't have fun with the person that you love, could you imagine yourself in a long-term relationship with them?

The old saying *laughter is the best medicine* actually holds a lot of truth to it. Being able to laugh heartily is a sign of happiness, and if laughter is something that you share a lot of in your relationship, that's a sign that your relationship is a happy one. Among the benefits that you stand to derive from having a sense of humor in your relationship include:

- **It Makes You Feel Physically Much Better** - Have you ever noticed how good you feel after a good laugh? How your spirits have just lifted and suddenly things don't seem so bad? Laughter is one of the most healing experiences we can go through as a human being, and it can physically do wonders for you better than any modern day medicine can. It releases endorphins in your body, which is the body's natural feel-good chemical, lowers your blood pressure, puts you in a relaxed state and even helps to lower stress.

- **It Lowers Your Inhibitions** - It's hard to feel defensive, angry or on the edge when you're feeling good and laughing. Especially if you're doing it with your partner, which is why humor is a much better situation diffuser than irony ever will be.

- **It Helps to Improve Your Communication** - Want to improve your communication between you and your partner? Use humor and laughter to do it. When a situation is tense and you think it's not going well, sometimes, a well-timed appropriate joke can help to break the tension and bring a smile to your partner's face. When you learn to laugh together about some of the challenges that go on in your life, it can sometimes help to put things into perspective, and even provide you with a creative solution you might not otherwise have thought of in your otherwise tense situation.

- **It Can Bring Back the Excitement In Your Relationship** - Things can often feel boring and stagnant after a while in a long term relationship. Especially if you or your partner are the kinds of people who often need excitement once in a while to keep things interesting. Having to deal with problems and challenges that go along with being in a relationship can sometimes take its toll. Well, guess what, laughter can help with that too. Not only does sharing these moments that make you laugh help to bring you closer together as a couple, but it can also even remind you of why you were attracted to your partner in the first place, and perhaps even make you fall in love with them all over again.

- **It Adds Another Layer of Intimacy** - Sharing inside jokes that no one else but you and your partner understand adds another layer of intimacy to your relationship. It's that knowledge of the special connection that you share, almost like a secret world that only the two of you know about, and when you look at each other, a smile, nod or wink can instantly create a surge of affection.

- **Helps to Restore Positivity in Your Relationship** - Not only does laughter help to diffuse difficult situations in your relationship, but it can also help to diffuse negative emotions too. It is impossible to feel that cloud of negativity when you're sharing a good laugh together.

- **Good Times Become Even Better** - Good times are made even better when there's laughter in the mix. Think about the moments when you and your partner were having a good time, and when you shared several laughs together, how much better those moments felt. You could look back for years to come and those memories would still bring a smile to your face. It gives you good stories to reminisce about too, when you say, "*Hey, remember that time when we…*" and laughing together all over again is only going to strengthen your bond even more.

CHAPTER 14: SKILL #14 – DON'T NEGLECT THE SEXUAL ASPECT

The sexual aspect of a relationship can cause a lot of worry and anxiety for many. Thanks to social media and movies and the unrealistic expectations they have set for romantic relationships, the pressure to perform in the bedroom can be overwhelming. Without proper communication going on, a relationship can quickly break down in the bedroom thanks to stress, anxiety, worry, and the fear that you're not living up to your partner's expectations.

Anxiety Over Sexual Relationships

Couples who are dealing with sexual intimacy issues are often susceptible to experiencing anxiety and fear, along with a wide range of worries that accompany those emotions. Among the things that may be running through a person's head when they worry about their intimate relationships include:

- They worry about being judged by their partner

- They suffer from low self-esteem and constantly find themselves worried about everything

- They constantly need to be reassured, sometimes on a daily basis and no matter how much your partner does his or her best to reassure you, it never feels like it is enough.

- They are unable to enjoy the sexual aspect of their relationship because they are more worried about whether they doing it right and whether they're satisfying you enough.

- They find it difficult to believe that their partner is happy with the sexual aspect of the relationship, despite the reassurance.

- They may find it difficult to be intimate because they are so full of worry.

- They experience a decrease in their sex drive as a direct result of that stress and worry.

Are you or your partner experiencing any of the symptoms or signs above? Then what you could be dealing with is sexual relationship anxiety. If left unchecked, this anxiety will only lead to mistrust and the inability to connect with your partner in the bedroom the way that you should as a couple. Sexual relationship anxiety can put a lot of pressure and stress on both people in the relationship, not just the one who is living with it, but also the one that has to deal with the one who has it. Excessive worry can lead to destructive relationship behaviors and over a prolonged period, it can cause the relationship to break down because one or both parties feel like they are not able to deal with the stress of it all anymore.

How to Recognize the Signs That Your Partner Is Suffering from Sexual Relationship Anxiety

Anxiety is an emotional state of being, and this means that different individuals will experience anxiety in different ways. If you suspect that you or your partner could be dealing with this, some common tell-tale signs to look out for include difficulty expressing their emotions. Common words that could possibly be expressed by your partner if he or she is going through anxiety would be worry, fear, dread, apprehension, distress, overwhelmed, pressure, stress, being on edge, and more. If they regularly express these emotions which are followed by signs of physical distress, that will signal to you that something is not right, because thought patterns like these are very commonly expressed by those who are dealing with anxiety.

If your partner is constantly expressing that they are feeling overwhelmed, that is something you need to take seriously because it is a symptom of anxiety. They feel overwhelmed because again, it is linked back to how they obsessed and overthink almost everything. You would be surprised that they can obsess even about the smallest, possible detail which may seem insignificant to you. Things like they feel that they're not good kissers, or that their body is not as perfect as they want it to be, or even that they feel they are not good in bed for example. As a result of overthinking, they get worked up and feel that they are unable to cope because they are not able to think straight and think rationally in the situation.

Anxiety over sexual relationships is a very real problem that is not to be taken lightly. Anxiety, in general, is an actual mental health issue that should never be dismissed with statements such as "it's all in your head." Anxiety is a serious issue that requires serious help.

What You Can Do to Help Your Partner Through It

Improving communication overall includes being able to communicate about the sexual aspect of your relationship. You may find that talking about all the other issues that take place is much easier than having to talk about your sex life. Yes, it may be a tough conversation to have, but if you're going to improve your overall communication as a couple, this is something you're going to have to learn to talk about too.

When your partner is dealing with sexual relationship anxiety, they are constantly worried and fearful. These are the two primary emotions that they are feeling. This constant state of worry and fear makes them less aware and unable to tune in to the needs of their partner because they are unable to focus on anything except their own worries and fears. When they are in this state, they find it difficult to trust and connect with anyone, even their partners. They may even feel that you are not being there for them in the way that they need because they are not thinking clearly.

When your partner is going through a moment like this, do your best to approach the situation calmly so you can help them to calm down. Avoid being equally emotional, because that could just escalate the situation when they are already in a highly emotional state of mind. You need to remain calm and steady before attempting to calm your partner down. Encourage them to talk to you about what they are feeling. The best thing for you to do in this situation would be to approach your partner with kindness and empathy (emotional intelligence comes into play here again). Remind them that you are not going anywhere, and if they need someone to talk to, encourage them to trust you enough to open up. It can be difficult to remain positive when things are difficult and challenging, so what you can do to help is to keep reminding yourself that your partner is only acting this way because of their sexual relationship anxiety, and this is not who they really are.

Other things you can do to reassure your partner and improve communication in the bedroom include:

- Creating a safe space to talk about things in a way that allows both of you to be comfortable enough to open up

- Showing your partner respect and support

- Notice what is important to them, what they need and make that a priority.

- Be genuine with your compliments and reassurances, so your partner knows that you're not just saying that because you're trying to get things to go your way in the bedroom.

- Open up to *them* about the way that *you feel.* Share your own worries, fears and needs so that they know they are not the only ones going through this alone.

CHAPTER 15: SKILL #15 – GETTING SOME SPACE

It is easy to lose yourself in a romantic relationship. Being caught up in the romance, trying to please your partner and keep them happy and wanting to spend as much time around them as possible can make you forget what life was like *before* you ventured into the relationship. You could easily get caught up in wanting to do all the things that your partner loves to do that you eventually neglect your own interests over time.

Why it becomes easy to lose ourselves in another person is because their happiness can take priority over ours - especially in the beginning. Because we love them, we want to do everything we can to make them happy and that becomes our number one priority. In doing so, we forget that there are other aspects of our lives that bring us meaning and happiness, even before we found our partners.

Why Getting Space Is Important

Especially when you live with your partner, it is important to find some time to do things independently and on your own. Neglecting the things that you like to do - hobbies, interests, passions, and activities - puts you in a dangerously unhealthy relationship. What's going to happen when your partner isn't around? You're going to find yourself completely at a loss, possibly even losing a sense of who you are, which has often happened with a lot of relationships where couples rely too heavily on each other.

The healthiest relationships are the ones where the couples are able to find a balance. They have common shared interests which allow them to bond and grow together as a couple, but they also have other interests which are independent of just themselves. These are the couples who enjoy each other's company, but at the same time are perfectly happy and content to enjoy their own company every now and then. It is important in every relationship that you maintain a sense of independence because:

- **You Need to Maintain Your Individuality -** If you're always so consumed by just the things that your partner loves to do, you're losing a lot of what makes you unique. The special qualities about yourself are part of the reason why your partner fell in love with you in the first place. It is part of your identity and who you are as a person. Maintaining a relationship with yourself is just as important as maintaining a relationship with another person. If you don't get to know yourself, you will never be able to love yourself.

- **You Are Able to Contribute More to Your Relationship -** You may be part of a relationship, but you are also your own person, and the individual qualities that make you great are what you contribute to making your relationship even better. When you're comfortable and happy with who you are as a person, you'll realize that you have so much more to offer. You don't need another individual to make you whole because *you are already whole enough.* Having your significant other in your life is just adding another element which brings you more happiness because now you have someone to share your life with.

- **It Keeps Your Relationship Alive -** If you're only going to be consumed by your partner's likes and interests, pretty soon you'll find that you have quickly run out of things to talk about. Especially in a long-term relationship. It may be more fun to do things with your partner, but when you push yourself out of your comfort zone, you'll gain an amazing new sense of freedom that you forgot was once there. You used to indulge in your activities and hobbies once upon a time before you found your partner, and when you continue doing that, perhaps even picking up new activities and interests along the way, you'll have even more things to share and talk about with your partner.

- **It Helps You Maintain Your Confidence -** When you become far too reliant on someone else to do things, you could lose your sense of confidence along the way. When you suddenly find yourself in a situation where you may have to do certain things alone, it suddenly feels difficult to engage in these activities with confidence. That can happen when you make someone else your focus, and what a lot of couples fail to realize is this can be a cause for the deterioration in their relationship. You feel bound to your partner for the wrong reasons, and sometimes you may even be afraid to leave a bad relationship because you don't want to find yourself alone again. This is why it is important to maintain your own independence, to create some space every now and then from your partner to do your own thing. It reminds you that you are capable of being on your own *and* in a healthy relationship, and you're capable of thriving in both situations.

- **You Need to Work On Your Own Happiness -** You owe it to yourself to work on your own happiness. If you rely on external forces for your happiness - and this includes your partner - you will find it hard to hold onto that happiness, especially when those sources are not around. Happiness needs to come from within and to do that, you need to work on yourself. When you feel genuinely happy, you're less stressed and tense, which then reduces the arguments that might occur. Your happiness should never be put in the hands of someone else, what your partner should be is *added joy*, instead of being the only reason for that happiness. The happiness that comes from within is the one that is going to last forever, and when you can bring that happiness into your relationship and share it with your partner, that's when the relationship grows stronger and flourishes.

While it is natural to want to share everything about your life with your partner, it is important to realize that not *everything* needs to be shared. In fact, having time away from each other and missing each other will only serve to make you appreciate your partner even more when you do reunite again.

CHAPTER 16: SKILL #16 – SETTING GOALS TOGETHER

A goal can set you down a very powerful path. As a couple, creating shared goals to work towards is one of the most powerful exercises you could do to improve not just your connection, but your communication. Working on shared goals together can be fun, especially because there is nothing better than doing things and sharing successful accomplishments with the person that you love.

Goals help to turn that everything you envision as a couple into a reality. Every couple wants to see their relationship going somewhere, and setting goals to work towards will help give you something to focus on.

What Exactly Is a Goal?

A goal is defined as a desire to achieve a result which you have envisioned in your mind. Think about all the things you had planned to do, especially as a couple, but haven't quite gotten around to doing them just yet. Could that be because you didn't have a goal in mind and an action plan to help you get to that desired outcome? A goal helps you stay on track because it reminds you why you got started to begin with.

Goals give you the focus, the knowledge, and the ability to organize both your time and resources so you are making the most out of every waking moment of the day. It gives you perspective in your life and helps you shape the decisions that you make from this point moving forward as a couple. Goal setting with your partner is even more fulfilling and rewarding because you know that you're not doing this alone. Having that support in the form of your partner can help to motivate and fuel your desire to succeed and vice versa.

Why Is It Important to Set Goals as a Couple?

Creating a shared vision and goals for yourselves, and as a couple is important. If you've ever found yourself in past relationships where you and your partner were on completely different pages, you'll know just how stressful it can be and what a strain it can be on a relationship. Or perhaps envision a moment when you've set a goal for what you want to achieve out of a relationship but along the way you struggled and felt frustrated because you felt you weren't receiving the support that you needed from your partner. Not being on the same page with you about your goal probably made it that much harder to communicate, which only increased the sense of frustration which was being felt.

For a relationship to survive and thrive in the long term, goal setting as a couple is something that is absolutely a necessity. Without goals, you may quickly find that your relationship loses a sense of purpose or direction along the way, especially when it reaches a point where it stagnates and doesn't feel like it is moving forward in the way that you hoped. Without that sense of purpose, a relationship can quickly crack under the strain.

How to Start Setting Goals as A Couple

Setting goals as a couple is about creating a vision that you share together and then making a commitment to achieve that vision. Setting goals as a couple is not at all complicated, and in fact, here are some simple but effective strategies to help you get started:

- **Defining the Areas of Importance -** There's a lot of things going on in a relationship, and while you may be tempted to tackle all these areas, try to take it one step at a time. Goal setting should start in the areas which matter the most to both of you as a couple. These areas could be for example marriage, family, finances, kids, or even buying your first home together. It can be anything that you want, as long as it is an area that you think is important to your relationship.

- **Talk About It and Write It Down -** Set some time to sit down and have a discussion about what goals you and your partner hope to get out of the relationship. Write down each goal that you have (ask your partner to do the same), and then compare the goals which you have written down and see if you've got anything in common. If there are different goals that you both would like to achieve, brainstorm what you can do to meet each other halfway, or help each other to realize these goals so both parties are happy and satisfied with the outcome.

- **Keep an Open Mind -** It is only natural that you and your partner are bound to have goals which are different. You're two very different people, with different perspectives and visions about where you see the relationship going. Keep an open mind when comparing goals with your partner and communicate with each other about why you think a particular goal is important. Understanding and listening to each other's point of view show that you are not dismissive towards each other's needs. Some of your partner's goals may not have been something that you would have initially considered, and some of your goals may not have been things that they would have considered.

- **Reflecting On the Goals You've Set -** Once you and your partner have finalized the goals that you would like to begin working on, spend a couple of minutes just reflecting on your goals. Take a good, long look at the goals which you have in front of you and map out the next steps which are needed moving forward to work towards achieving these goals together as a team.

- **Time for Action -** Next, it's time to work together with your partner on devising a plan of action. This is another great opportunity to work on communicating with each other as you begin to talk about how you're going to work through this process together. The action plan that you settle on should be aligned with your goals. If your goal, for example, commits to doing an activity of interest once a month to work on strengthening your bond as a couple, then the action plan should include a list of activities to do, when during the month this should happen and what are the ground rules for this activity. The rules could be no use of mobile phones during that time so you can really enjoy the time you spend with each other. Your action plan does not have to be comprehensive to begin with, it is just to get you started. As you go along, you can add more steps and more actions as ideas start flowing into your mind.

By setting these goals together as a couple, it helps to put the goals in a larger context and gives you a sense of purpose as a couple. The shared victories and successes which you accomplish along the way will give you something to celebrate over, and it also helps to pinpoint which areas of your relationship need working on so you can improve moving forward.

CHAPTER 17: SKILL #17 – DON'T' HOLD ONTO ANGER

If there is one emotion that is present and exists in everyone, it is anger. It is considered one of our core emotions, like happiness. It happens even to the best people. While anger is a natural emotion, it becomes a problem when it happens more frequently than it should, especially in romantic relationships. It becomes an even *bigger problem* when one or both partners refuse to let go of that anger and move on from it.

Have you ever had moments where you recalled an argument or a confrontation you had, and the mere thought of it just makes your blood boil all over again? That's what anger can do. It makes you hold onto grudges, makes it hard to forgive, let go and move on. Prolonged anger in any relationship, not just the romantic ones, can lead to unhappiness, years of not talking to one another and cause relationships to be ruined over matters which are often not worth it at all. The problem with anger in some people is that they find it hard to let go.

Why Do We Feel Angry?

There could be several reasons why we feel angry. Since each individual is unique, everyone is going to have different triggers which cause anger to spring forth. Some examples of what could be anger triggers in a romantic relationship include the following:

- When you experience unfair treatment
- When you feel you are being treated unkindly
- When you have been lied to
- When promises are broken
- When you feel you are being disrespected
- When you feel powerless or helpless to put a stop to something
- When your partner doesn't seem to "listen" or do the things you expect them to
- When you're disappointed
- When you feel neglected
- When you can't come to an agreement during an argument
- During an argument
- When things are not going your way

There could be so many possible scenarios and situations that could cause a person to get angry or upset about it. Being able to identify your triggers is how you learn to recognize the factors in your relationship that often cause you to get angry. Once you realize what causes you to get angry, the next step is to understand just how big of a problem it is.

When Does Anger Become a Problem in A Relationship?

While anger is not uncommon and is bound to happen in every relationship, there are several indicators to look out for which signal when your anger may start to go from healthy to problematic. Some of these indicators include:

- You find it hard to let go of anger, even over the smallest of issues, and you let this anger simmer and boil within you until you explode once again and lash out at your partner.
- You find yourself feeling frustrated and sometimes depressed because of repressed anger issues which you may not even be aware of.
- You find it hard to have a happy, meaningful relationship because you constantly find yourself annoyed, frustrated, disgruntled and perhaps even snappy at even the smallest things.
- You hold onto grudges for a very long time because of that anger and you could end up going for days or weeks without speaking to your partner because of it.
- You find it hard to express your anger in healthy ways, preferring to let it bottle up inside you instead which leads to other emotional problems.
- Other people have told you that you have an anger problem, especially your partner.
- You always are pessimistic and negative because of your anger issues.

Often those who have an anger issue do not realize just how problematic it can be. Especially on the people who are closest to them. They don't understand the full extent of just how hurtful angry words and behavior patterns can be, especially for your partner who is around you the most. Dealing with someone who gets angry far too easily is an exhausting ordeal, constantly having to pacify them and soothe them takes up a lot of time and energy. Your partner will eventually grow weary of having to walk on eggshells around you because they don't want to do anything to set you off, and that, over time, will cause the relationship to break down and make communication difficult.

How to Start Learning to Let Go

It is important to realize that all that stuff you get angry about, the things that you're holding a grudge over, it is not worth it. What is *worth it,* however, is your partner. The person you love. The person who is there for you. That is what matters, not your anger. And it certainly isn't worth it to lose someone you love over anger.

The best thing that you could do for your relationship is to learn to let go. Don't expect your partner to "accept" your anger because this is who you are and this is part of your personality. That is entirely the wrong approach to use, and the only thing you are doing is making excuses to justify your behavior without having to do anything to change it. For the sake of your relationship, you are going to have to put in the effort to make a difference if you want to *see* a difference.

- **You Don't Need to Always Be Right -** There's no need for you to always be right and for one very simple reason. It's not worth it. By continuing to indulge in this behavior, you're not helping yourself or your anger issues. You are, in fact, making things much worse. Let go of the desire and the need to always be right. It will get easier over time too, and you'll feel a sense of satisfaction because deep down, you know that it is the right thing to do.

- **No More Room for Excuses -** The more excuses you make, the harder it will be for you to let go of your anger. There will always be a reason for you to *not* let it go. A reason to be angry, a reason to feel annoyed. There will always be a reason as long as you want it to be. Let go of the excuses and you will learn to let go of your anger eventually.

- **Do Activities Which Make You Happy -** The oldest and one of the most effective. People who struggle with anger issues have a lot of misery and unhappiness inside them. The antidote to that unhappiness is - you guessed it - happiness. Indulge in a passion or a hobby, throw yourself into an activity that you love. With a happier state of mind, it makes it easier to think with a clearer head, you don't get as worked up so easily anymore and it becomes much easier to learn how to control your anger issues.

- **Keep A Mood Journal -** One of the problems when it comes to anger is that you're so overwhelmed with all sorts of emotion that it all comes out all at once, especially when you have been keeping it bottled up for so long. Keeping a journal provides you with a safe and private place where you can express every feeling and emotion you have without the fear of being ridiculed or judged. More importantly, it is possible the safest outlet for you to release your feelings of anger with repercussions, without hurting anyone or yourself in the process, especially your partner.

- **Learning to Forgive -** Getting angry is easy. But forgiveness? Well, that's a different story. It takes great inner strength to forgive and be the bigger person, and it is going to take a lot of work, but it will well be worth it. It is a choice that you alone must make. It helps to remind yourself that this is someone you love and that alone should be enough of a reason for forgiveness.

CHAPTER 18: SKILL #18 – SINCERITY MATTERS

Communication is a process which takes a lot of work. *A lot of work.* If you're ever in any doubt about that, just remember the last time you and your partner had a conversation that you walked away from feeling extremely let down, heartbroken at being misunderstood, perhaps even feeling angry. How many times during those moments have you found yourself wishing that you could have communicated better with your partner and perhaps the outcome could have been completely different?

If there is one element which could change the way an entire conversation goes, it is sincerity. Couples often struggle to communicate with each other, especially during difficult conversations about challenging issues because sometimes sincerity is lacking. You may not be able to always control the way your partner communicates, but you *can control how you communicate*, and it starts with understanding why sincerity is such an important and necessary element of the communication process.

As human beings who are involved in a romantic relationship, we need two basic necessities to be happy. We need security, and we need to be able to trust the people that we are with. These two elements rely on our partner to play their part, and likewise, we need to do the same for them, and the way to do that is to be sincere in our relationships. Marianne Dainton, a relationship expert at the La Salle University in Philadelphia, explains that while sometimes little white lies are necessary to help maintain a balance in a relationship or to protect our loved ones, not everyone is in agreement with Dainton's theory. That's because, in reality, there is no one who is in a relationship that will ever say they are okay being lied to. *No one.* Lies have been the downfall of many relationships.

Relationship Happiness Boils Down to Sincerity

There are many factors which contribute to the success of a relationship. Empathy, respect, compatibility, communication, honesty, love (of course) and the most underrated quality of all - *sincerity.* A lot of relationships fall apart not because they have fallen out of love with their partner (although sometimes that may be the case), but because the couples felt a lack of sincerity in the relationship.

When a lack of sincerity exists in a relationship, it creates a distance between you and your partner. People can sense when someone isn't being sincere, no matter how well they think they are hiding that fact, but remember that your body language will eventually always give you away. It causes communication problems when two people aren't able to freely express how they feel about each other, and try to cover it up instead with lies and untruths. Hiding things from the people that you love will never bring any benefit, even though you may believe it is for their own good. Once trust has been severed between two people, it is very hard to repair the damage and earn their trust back again.

How to Start Building a Relationship Based on Sincerity

The foundation of a happy relationship cannot be built if one, or both people in that relationship don't fully understand just how valuable sincerity is. What it means to be sincere is that you are always making a choice to act with honesty and truthfulness at all times. That's all it takes. Be honest with yourself, being truthful to who you are, what motivates you, what you value and always choosing to be truthful about it with your partner. This is what sincerity in a relationship means.

If you think that a lack of sincerity could be a problem that your relationship is dealing with right now that's potentially hindering communication between you and your partner, it's time to do something about it. The situation can still be fixed when acted on quickly enough, and here's how you start building a relationship based on sincerity:

- **It's the Promises You Keep That Make a Difference** - Each time you're about to make a promise to your partner, think of this old saying: *Don't make promises that you can't keep.* Making promises to your partner feels good, to see the smile on their face, but each time you make a promise that you can't keep, the disappointment leaves a little scar within them that chips away at their trust in you. Broken promises hurt, a lot and each promise that gets broken will make it harder for your partner to trust you the next time you make another promise, even when you're sincere about it.

- **Back Your Words Up with Actions** - Words alone are not enough to convince your partner of your sincerity if there's no action to back it up. Another apt saying which sums it all up nicely is *actions speak louder than words*. If all you're doing is using words to make your partner feel better but nothing ever gets done, it's the same as making empty promises that you can't keep.

- **Don't Change Who You Are to Fit In** - You won't be able to put on an act forever. You and your partner are very different people, with different circumstances and different values. If you change who you are because you "think" it's what your partner is hoping for or wanting to see from you, that's not a good basis for building a sincere relationship. Your personality is what makes you who you are, and your partner is with you because they love you for *who you are.* You don't have to change just to feel like you fit in, so be sincere to yourself first before you can begin extending that same sincerity to your partner.

- **Don't Say Or Do Anything You Don't Feel Happy About** - If you're not entirely comfortable doing or saying something, then don't say it. Even if it may be what your partner wants to hear from you. Sincerity doesn't exist if you're pretending for the sake of making someone else happy. They may be happy, but you won't be, not in the long run especially. If you do something for your partner, it should be because you *want to*, not because you feel like you're being forced into it. If you're not entirely comfortable doing or saying something, then let your partner know right from the very beginning. They'll understand.

- **Expressing Gratitude Genuinely -** You know that you feel grateful for your partner and appreciate everything that they do. How do you let them know though? Do you just say how grateful you are for them? Or do you show them how grateful you are through your actions? Don't wait for them to have to ask for something, just do it. Help them out around the house, make a busy day less stressful, buy them flowers for no reason. That way, when you tell them how grateful you are to have them in your life, there is sincerity in it because it was backed up by actions.

CHAPTER 19: SKILL #19 – PRODUCTIVE CONFLICT HELPS

Nobody likes arguing with their partner. If we all could avoid arguments at all, we would. Some couples argue more than others do, and while arguments generally have a negative element associated to it, but there is such a thing as productive conflict, where arguing may actually be a good thing for your relationship.

In fact, in a study conducted by Joseph Grenny and David Maxfield conducted an online study entitled *Able Arguers* in 2012 which discovered that the happiest couples were the ones who engaged in healthy conflict. They were 10 times more likely in fact, to have a relationship that was happy as opposed to the couples who preferred to ignore or avoid arguments altogether.

According to Maxfield, who is co-authored follow up books to the *Crucial Conversations: Tools for Talking When Stakes are High* books (which were also co-authored by Grenny), the reason these couples are happier was not because arguing was good, but rather because they understand that disagreements are unavoidable and ignoring them is not going to make things any better. The difference was in *how* the couples chose to handle these disagreements. The couples, according to the study conducted, who handled these arguments in a productive way using honesty, love, respect, and by being frank were the ones who experienced a lot more success than the ones who did not.

Grenny and Maxfield also discovered in their study that 4 out of 5 individuals claimed that poor communication was responsible or played a role in the failure of their last relationship. Half the respondents also claimed poor communication was largely responsible for their failed relationship and dissatisfaction which was experienced in the relationship.

Why Productive Conflict Is Good for Your Relationship

Now, you may be wondering how arguments can turn out to be a good thing for your relationship. Here is why handling a conflict in a productive way can be more beneficial for your relationship than you think:

- **Productive Conflict Enables You to Communicate Your Needs -** Arguing provides you with an opportunity to communicate your needs to your partner about what's making you frustrated. Arguments only become unhealthy when you allow negative traits like maliciousness, spitefulness, bitterness, and cruelty get into the mix. What a lot of couples don't realize is that arguments could be handled completely differently and in a mature manner. Use this as an opportunity instead to communicate with your partner and explain to them about why you're feeling the way that you are.

- **Productive Conflict Prevents You From Lashing Out -** You may not like having arguments with your partner, but believe it or not, it is much better than keeping everything bottled up inside. The problem with keeping in all that anger and frustration is that it tends to explode in the most inappropriate moments at times. To prevent this situation is exactly why productive conflicts must be addressed, to keep you or your partner from lashing out in anger later on which could end up being much worse.

- **Productive Conflict Helps You Discover Motives -** According to Dr. Laura VanderDrift, who is an associate professor of psychology based at the Syracuse University in the College of Arts and Sciences, when a couple argues in the right manner, it can actually serve to strengthen their relationship instead of breaking it down. The right manner here being arguing without any form of criticism, contempt or even defensiveness, in other words, engaging in productive conflict. Productive conflict can help you resolve and get to the heart of the matter as to why you're having a conflict of interest, which then helps you discover what your partner's motives may be. Being able to engage in productive conflict will actually help you discover and perhaps learn something new about your partner that you may not have realized prior to this.

- **Productive Conflict Can Help to Save Your Relationship -** A relationship is a lot more likely to break down if you and your partner choose to ignore the serious issues at hand rather than hash it out and try to resolve the problem. If you're always worried about getting into arguments and trying to avoid conflict, what you don't realize is that this creates an even bigger problem because the underlying issue is not being addressed. The so-called "elephants in the room" is the one that is going to be the cause of your relationship falling apart, not productive conflict.

- **Productive Conflict Can Lead to a Change for the Better -** See arguments as a sign that something needs to change. If everything was going well the way that it should, and nothing needed changing, there would be no reason to have an argument, right? Productive conflict can be a good thing because it can push you and your partner towards having a healthy discussion about the changes that need to take place in your relationship for the better and what can you do about it. Good conflict makes you think about what you can do to improve the situation instead of taking a defensive, argumentative stance against it. If you and your partner started viewing productive conflict as an opportunity to make positive changes, your entire perception about arguments will change and you will no longer actively try to avoid conflict any longer.

CHAPTER 20: SKILL #20 – DEVELOPING DIPLOMATIC DIALOGUE SKILLS

The words that you use during your communication process can have a big impact on the outcome. It isn't just about the tone of voice, but the *words* that you say which is going to have the biggest impact of all on your partner. For example, during a disagreement, you may not be shouting at your partner, but if the words that you utter during those moments are dripping with contempt, harsh and just plain insulting, you those words end up hurting your partner more than if you were actively yelling at them.

This brings us to Skill #20, learning how to develop diplomatic dialogue skills when you communicate with your partner (or anyone else in your life for that matter).

What Does Diplomatic Communication Mean?

Someone who has developed the ability to communicate in a diplomatic manner is someone who has mastered the art of being able to get their messages across the way that they intended and convince the people who are listening to make the changes that they want, *without* causing any harm or damage to the relationship. How are they able to do this so effectively?

For one thing, they don't resort to manipulation to do it, but rather achieve this outcome by communicating with respect, compassion, kindness, and reason. They treat the person with whom they're speaking to as an equal, and they are honest about the things that they say. One might even say that they are *brutally* honest. They don't aim to misrepresent the truth when they communicate, which fosters the element of trust. No matter who they may be speaking to, they always try to interact with the person in a positive manner, making them feel like an important part of the conversation.

Bringing These Diplomatic Communication Techniques into Your Relationship

These are all wonderful traits which you can start bringing into your communication style with your partner and see what an improvement it can make in the way that you talk to each other.

- **Be Mindful of Your Choice of Words -** It is *very important* to be careful about the words that you use. Just one wrong word is all it takes to make a conversation go south and evoke a negative outcome or response. Your choice of words is important because of people's perceptions. Political consultant Frank Luntz even made this aspect a subtitle in his book entitled *Words that Work*, in which he summed it up perfectly by stating that *it is not about what you say, it is about what people hear.* When you're engaged in a productive conflict discussion with your partner, for example, avoid using aggressive words like *you must, you have to, never, always* which foster an element of negativity. Instead, replace those words with more diplomatic language, such as *why don't* *you consider, I think it might be better, have you ever considered perhaps...* Do you see how just a change of words puts an entirely different spin on the same message? To keep a conversation diplomatic between you and your partner, think about the words you want to use, then re-think about how you could make those words better, then *think yet again* about whether these are the best choice of words to use to achieve the outcome that you want.

- **Be Respectful -** It cannot be stressed enough how important it is to constantly be respectful throughout a conversation if you want to keep the peace. Respect goes a long way, and when you make your partner feel respected like their opinions and ideas are valued, you will see just how different the interaction is going to become. A little bit of an emotional intelligence exercise, here again, is to use empathy and put yourself in their shoes. If they were speaking to you disrespectfully, would you be inclined to just sit there and continue to listen without feeling any kind of negative emotion towards them? Highly unlikely. In fact, that is the quickest way to turn an argument bad, by being disrespectful to your partner when you're having a conversation with them because what you're doing is showing them that you don't care about their feelings at all.

- **Listen and Be Open-Minded -** Communication works both ways, as we've already realized by now. For diplomatic conversations to occur, you're going to have to become an active listener and maintain an open mind. When you don't listen to your partner, you're indirectly telling them that you are not respecting their feelings or their needs - that you don't want to accept their point of view because it may be different from what you want. A key trait of being a diplomatic communicator is to never blurt out the first thing that comes into your head, because that's often how you end up putting your foot in your mouth, especially during a conversation where emotions are running high. Diplomatic communicators actively avoid saying things that they might regret later on, which is why they put a lot of careful thought into their choice of words. Always be a listener first before you become a speaker, and keep an open mind about every conversation, even if you may not necessarily agree with what you hear.

- **Timing is Everything -** Timing matters just as much as what you say. There is a time and a place for everything, and diplomatic communicators know this. If your partner has just come home after having a very hard day at work and they're feeling tense and stressed, would now be a good time to bother them about a task that you've asked them to do but they haven't quite got around to it yet? No, definitely not. Communicating diplomatically means picking the time and the place to hold certain discussions because choosing to bring up something at the wrong time is also going to be hurtful towards your partner, since it shows that you're not considering their needs at that time.

- **No Emotional Reactions -** One thing a diplomatic communicator never does is to react emotionally during a conversation. That's because they know it is impossible to be respectful or tactful during a conversation if your emotions are getting the best of you. This is another diplomatic dialogue skill you need to start practicing with your partner. If you're not feeling calm and composed, then it may not necessarily be the right time to have the conversation that you want.

CHAPTER 21: SKILL #21 - ORGANIZING ROMANTIC MEETINGS

Almost every relationship begins through some elements of romance, and most couples expect their lovers, co-parents or best friends to continue to be romantic in the relationship. However, sometimes the pressures and demands of life can phase romance out and cause the relationship to evolve and lean towards being more functional than romantic.

Balancing the demands of life and maintaining romance in a relationship can be hard on couples. Throw kids in the equation and the strain becomes worse. Nonetheless, if managed well, relationships can be a source of joy and satisfaction to couples.

Marriage therapist Marcia N. Berger said, *"the art of marriage is really the art of keeping up to date with your partner, of staying on track with your own and each other's life goals as they emerge, exist, and change. It is about supporting each other and staying connected emotionally, intellectually, physically, and spiritually."*

How can couples keep up with all that? By organizing Romantic Meetings.

Benefits of Romantic Meetings

If you and your partner talk daily and wonder why this is important for your relationship, the answer is so that you can intentionally go deeper into discussions that you would most likely brush off when you are pressed for time or do not feel like addressing on the spot.

Sometimes, what we say and what we mean when we say certain things may not be represented accurately. This can turn into unnecessary misunderstandings that build up emotional stressors over time, especially when we refuse to sit down and discuss it because it was inconvenient or not important at the time. This will eventually reflect through our behavior around each other, affecting both romantic behavior and communication patterns.

A Romantic Meeting can address both functional and emotional needs of a couple. It enables couples to be on the same page and ensures that your relationship steers towards the right direction. This contributes to a more harmonious and orderly home. As you talk things out with your partner during the meeting, you will be able to weed out issues that were not really issues in the first place and make space to discuss real challenges and problems. Removing unnecessary doubt also allows both of you the mental space to be romantic around each other and be intentional about it. Intentional - that is the key to romance.

How to Start Planning Romantic Meetings

Here are some ideas to help you get started on planning for Romantic Meetings:

Set a time

Some couples work best with weekly meetings, while some prefer only once a month. Pick a schedule that suits both of you and adjust the time according to your preferences.

Set the tone

This involves picking a romantic place to dine, or even a familiar place that both of you have fond memories of. The tone of the meeting is not only set by the location but both of you. Dress the part and bring a positive vibe to the meeting. During the meeting, try to use uplifting and encouraging words instead of criticizing your partner. Please, by all means, flirt and compliment one another as much as you can.

Minimize Distractions

Put your phones away. You have come so far as to set aside time. Make the most of your time together and give each other your full attention. Try to pick a place that both of you are also comfortable to talk and hear each other out. Distractions like sound, television or movement can act as stressors that defeat the purpose of the meeting.

Sit together

Try not to sit across from each other as this can seem confrontational during discussions. Sitting side by side can feel as if both of you are headed in the same direction, together. This gives a sense of unity and the physical closeness can also ignite some romantic feelings.

Write notes

Whatever your partner has to say is important. If you are not the kind of person who pays attention to detail, or has good memory, write them down. You will be talking about to-dos and setting dates for important events. You do not want your partner thinking that what they have to say is unimportant to you.

Own the meeting

The meeting is for both of you. It is important to understand the goal of meeting together; to build the relationship and rekindle romantic feelings. Give equal time to each other to express thoughts and feelings. If you are usually more verbal and dominant than the other, dial down a little and let your partner speak. Try to work past awkward moments and be true to your aim; better communication, better relationship.

Just the two of you

If it wasn't clear in the beginning, this meeting is for the both of you only. Try not to bring kids or pets that would be a cause for distraction and make you feel more reserved about expressing your thoughts.

Parts of Romantic Meetings

Marcia Berger suggests planning for weekly meetings with your partner that consists of four parts: Appreciation, Chores, Plan for Good Times, and Problems or Challenges.

The Appreciation part of the meeting involves the expression of gratitude towards your partner. These expressions should be specific, 100% positive and touch on behavioral or character traits that you like about your partner. This gives them positive reinforcement and the confidence to continue certain behaviors.

The allocation of chores can be brought up during these meetings as well. Couples can make to-do lists and discuss what else needs to be done. This part of the meeting is meant for couples to work things through together, however, if things get heated and the couple cannot agree on a decision, the discussion is brought to the Problems or Challenges part of the meeting. They can also opt to bring it up in the next Romantic Meeting.

Thirdly, Berger encourages couples to Plan for Good Times. This involves scheduling date nights or family activities. It gives couples something to look forward to and plan together. This time can also surface common interests or help partners understand each other's likes or dislikes better.

Lastly, discussing Problems or Challenges allows couples to address issues, conflicts or changes in the relationship. This could involve anything from individual insecurities, to who should attend your child's concert or even problems at work. Be determined to make this a safe space for both of you to address concerns without being defensive or judgmental.

Romantic Meetings can look differently for different people, and it is okay to change the format of the meeting to suit both your needs over time. Feel free to improvise and be creative around your meetings so they don't turn into a boring routine.

CHAPTER 22: THE 7-DAY CHALLENGE - WORKSHOP TO BETTER COMMUNICATION

Most couples expect to quickly 'bounce back' to their honeymoon feelings after a Romantic Meeting, but that isn't always the case. Habits, behaviors, communication, and trust is built over time and it varies from one person to another. You probably have people warned you that relationships gradually evolve over time and it takes so much more energy to maintain it, but most of us believe things like that will not happen to us.

The fact that you are reading this means that something has triggered your need or desire to repair or improve your communication with your partner. It also means you are not entirely happy with what both of you have right now. This is absolutely normal for almost every relationship, and it also absolutely okay to feel that way. But before you diagnose or think the worst of your situation, give your partner and yourself a week to figure things out and work towards better communication.

Try this 7-Day Challenge to improve communication with your partner.

Day 1: Reflect and be honest

In the previous chapter, we mentioned the power of being intentional. This first day requires you to be intentional about looking inward and realizing that it takes both time and consistency to make a relationship work. It isn't about what you can do to magically make all communication woes disappear, but how you can work on it.

Be real about the change that you want to see in yourself. Ask yourself what needs to give, in order for the relationship to be stronger. Being very honest about your why you are going through communication problems and why you behave the way you do will help you be the best version of yourself and inevitably contribute to better communication.

Day 2: Commit to one change

No matter what point you are in your relationship, you are definitely already aware of some of your partner's likes and dislikes. You know their pet peeves and can probably identify what gets on their nerves. Whatever they are, pay attention to them and try your best to change or stop doing certain things that can trigger that. If they like certain things that you do, try to make them more frequent. If there is something that you can do to make them feel better, why not? For example, if you know they enjoy getting little notes of appreciation, drop them more often. If your partner dislikes you leaving the toilet seat down, lift it up when you remember. Little steps like these can go a long way in developing romantic feelings and trust.

Day 3: Say 'Hi' like it's a big deal

Greet your partner like you greet your best friend. Surely, you are happier to have your partner around than when they are away. Make a big deal to acknowledge their presence and express how much they mean to you. We tend to take people we often see for granted, but greeting your partner in a more enthusiastic way can make them feel appreciated and can go a long way in steering your relationship in a different direction. Before you know it, you look forward to this new behavior and enjoy being around each other more.

Day 4: Talk about the bad stuff objectively

You probably won't be able to talk about arguments on the spot, but when both of you have calmed down, take time to hear each other out and be objective about the disagreement. What's valuable about this is that it allows both of you to have a more rational approach to your problems, and this gives both of you the opportunity to resolve the conflict and have closure.

Day 5: Gaze into each other's eyes

No talking and no touching. This seems a little funny, but looking into your partner's eyes builds emotional intimacy. Try this for 10 minutes and gradually increase the length of time. Once you are done, talk about what went through your minds and laugh about it. It will probably feel awkward at first, but doing this daily will help establish an emotional connection and perhaps lead to other kinds of intimacy.

Day 6: Compliment your partner and yourself

Do you find yourself silently adoring your partner? Well, it is worth expressing your admiration. A compliment can be about anything: the way he or she looks, the way they think, how they responded to a problem, or even how they match their clothes. Be genuine about it and try to find something different to complement each other every day. It strengthens your bond and even encourages your partner to repeat the behavior that you like.

We are always too preoccupied with pleasing other people that we tend to forget what we like about ourselves. Make time to recognize the things that you are proud of and give yourself a pat on the back. It is also okay to hug yourself. These are commonly used in therapy to help people who struggle with anxiety and depression. So, while you are complimenting your partner and making them feel good about themselves, give yourself some therapy as well.

Day 7: Ask questions

People change over time and your partner can too. Perhaps both of you are no longer the same people who fell in love years ago. Perhaps it is time to get to know each other again. Ask questions to discover new things about your partner and you'd be surprised to uncover things you have never realized about them. Treating each other like strangers can also ignite excitement and gives you the chance to fall in love with them all over again.

There are no fool proof ways to better communication, and as earlier mentioned, healing and building relationships take time. Some people get better within these 7 days, and some - with the consistent practice of the above - take a little longer. Be patient with each other and remember to be intentional about the things that you say and do.

REFERENCES:

- https://www.psychologytoday.com/us/blog/fulfillment-any-age/201206/the-12-ties-bind-long-term-relationships
- https://www.heysigmund.com/vulnerability-the-key-to-close-relationships/
- https://www.5lovelanguages.com/
- https://www.thepublicdiscourse.com/2015/12/15983/
- https://www.brides.com/story/body-language-in-relationships
- https://bestlifeonline.com/body-language-tells-every-single-person-should-know/
- https://www.skillsyouneed.com/ips/challenging-conversations.html
- https://www.huffingtonpost.com.au/entry/5-ways-using-your-phone-less-can-improve-your-relationship-and-how-to-do-it_us_55ad0662e4b0caf721b331b7
- https://psycnet.apa.org/record/2014-52280-001
- https://www.pewinternet.org/fact-sheet/mobile/
- https://goodmenproject.com/sex-relationships/approach-difficult-conversations-partner-fiff/
- https://www.yourtango.com/2019322672/daily-horoscopes-today-thursday-march-21-2019-zodiac-signs-astrology
- https://www.mydomainehome.com.au/judgment-bad-for-intimacy-in-relationships
- https://www.cheatsheet.com/health-fitness/how-laughter-can-improve-your-relationship.html/
- https://www.bedsider.org/features/1065-5-reasons-why-laughter-makes-relationships-even-better
- https://www.psychologytoday.com/us/blog/conscious-communication/201703/why-conflict-is-healthy-relationships
- https://www.josephgrenny.com/
- https://hbr.org/search?term=david+maxfield
- http://thecollege.syr.edu/people/faculty/pages/psy/machia-laura.html

- https://www.bustle.com/p/7-ways-arguing-benefits-your-relationship-according-to-experts-8268192

- https://www.prevention.com/sex/g20474958/7-steps-to-improve-your-marriage-in-just-one-week/

- https://www.artofmanliness.com/articles/how-and-why-to-hold-a-weekly-marriage-meeting/

- Ogolsky, B. G., & Bowers, J. R. (2013). A meta-analytic review of relationship maintenance and its correlates. *Journal of Social and Personal Relationships, 30*, 343-367.

CONCLUSION

Thank for making it through to the end of this book, let's hope it was informative and able to provide you with all of the tools you need to achieve your goals whatever they may be.

For better or worse, in both good and bad times, one constant remain - *couples always need each other.* Every couple goes through hard times, and sometimes even with good communication, you're going to have these challenges. However, good communication can help you overcome these situations much better because you and your partner will now know how to express yourselves openly and freely using all the right techniques and skills.

Finally, if you found this books useful in anyway, a review on Amazon is always appreciated!

Made in the USA
Lexington, KY
21 June 2019